PREACHING
THROUGH THE
CHRISTIAN YEAR
7

By the same author:

These are the Hymns
Cornish Bishop (with John Peart Binns)
The Study of Liturgy (contributor to)

Other Mowbray Sermon Outlines

Preaching Through the Christian Year
Series Editor: D. W. Cleverley Ford
Vols 4 & 6 by Fenton Morley
Vol. 5 by Robert Martineau

Preaching at the Parish Communion
Series 3 Service and Lectionary
Vol. 4 Gospels (Year One) by Hugh Fearn
Vol. 5 Gospels (Year Two) by Hugh Fearn
Vol. 6 Gospels, Epistles, Collects (Year One)
        by Frank Colquhoun
Vol. 7 Gospels, Epistles, Collects (Year Two)
        by D. W. Cleverley Ford

New Preaching from the New Testament
by D. W. Cleverley Ford

New Preaching from the Old Testament
by D. W. Cleverley Ford

Preaching on Special Occasions
by D. W. Cleverley Ford

Preaching Through the Acts of the Apostles
by D. W. Cleverley Ford

PREACHING THROUGH THE CHRISTIAN YEAR 7

Sermon Outlines for the Seasons of the Church's Year

Alan Dunstan

MOWBRAY
LONDON & OXFORD

ISBN 0 264 66421 3

First published 1980
by A. R. Mowbray & Co. Ltd
Saint Thomas House
Becket Street, Oxford OX1 1SJ

Reprinted 1983

Typeset by Oxford Publishing Services,
The Studio, Stratford Street, Oxford

Printed in Great Britain by
Biddles Ltd, Guildford, Surrey

To the Congregations
who have helped me to preach
and to the Students
whom I have helped to preach

CONTENTS

INTRODUCTION

To This Book

A book of sermons has one main purpose. It is to help other people preach their own sermons. There are doubtless still some who read sermons for their own edification, and are not themselves called to preach. But it is likely that most readers of this book will be preachers. The contents of the book are not, by intention, ready-made sermons. The value of a printed sermon is that it can give another preacher something to work on for himself — maybe a single thought, or a particular quotation.

There is something mummified about a printed sermon. The present preacher is in the habit of writing out every word of the sermons he proposes to preach. But he does not normally take his manuscript into the pulpit. He "goes through it" a number of times at home; and although he happens to have a photographic memory, what he says in the pulpit is not precisely what he has written. In any case, he will, on the spur of the moment shorten, amend or add to the material. This is one reason why he finds the written sermon slightly artifical. And there is another. His illustrations tend, in the main, to arise from contemporary events or local situations — which would often be too dated or too obscure to repeat in this volume.

Strictly speaking, the sermon is that which is delivered in the pulpit. It is not the manuscript used in its preparation, nor is it the manuscript reconstructed afterwards for the purpose of a book like this. The sermon is the word of God interpreted by a certain person to a certain congregation on a certain occasion. Before coming to Gloucester Cathedral, I preached on most Sundays for eight years at St Cross Church in Oxford. But I cannot preach the *same* sermons in Gloucester as I did at St Cross. The setting is different and the people are different, and although I may be preaching the same message, there are a whole number of reasons why it must be slanted differently. Of course I do not pretend that I never use old material. Most of us do this unconsciously; try writing a new Easter sermon without reference to what is in your file for this occasion, and you will be surprised at how much you have repeated yourself! We can all take comfort from the fact that the illustrious who write many books do the same thing. But I have found that if I want to use an 'old sermon' I must write it out afresh if it is going to live for me, and therefore for those who hear it. And there is always the possibility, to which I hope I am sensitive, that God will want me to speak rather differently on this theme from the last time in which I preached on it.

To Preaching

I write as one who believes in preaching. I see other means of communicating the Gospel — art, dialogue, drama and music, to name but a few — as partners rather than rivals to preaching. Preaching is unique, just as the other methods are unique. As an Anglican, I would lay equal stress on Word and Sacrament as means of grace. Sometimes our practice of this does not measure up to our boasting of it. But I believe that the presence of the living Lord is made real to us both in the breaking of the Word and in the breaking of the Bread.

For this reason, as well as the fact that this has seemed a particular calling for me, a large part of my ministry has been given to the preparation and delivery of sermons. I do not mean that I have necessarily agonised for long hours at my desk over each one. I do mean that directly a preaching engagement has been made, I have *begun* to think about it. Dr. Leonard Griffith, sometime Minister of the City Temple, used to set up files for a *year* — in which he would, from time to time, insert material appropriate to the subjects he had chosen. Not many of us could work so far ahead, nor would it be desirable for us to try — but it is a method that could be applied to a month or six weeks. To decide *what* we shall preach about on a particular occasion is often half the battle; and besides its many advantages, this discipline can help us not to ride too many hobby-horses.

There are three main strands to the preparation of a sermon — which we might call the theological, the social and the pastoral. The theological is concerned with the particular aspect of the

Word of God which is to be preached — and this will obviously require the use of commentaries and dictionaries. The second concerns the society to which and in which we preach — which involves a knowledge of how people live, of what questions they are really asking, of what problems they have to face, of what temptations most beset them. The pastoral is concerned with how the first is applied to the second — which involves the use of the media, but above all of the imagination. Because of all this, the itinerant preacher has a much more difficult role than the man who normally preaches to those whom he knows.

Most books on preaching urge us to write out our aim before we start, and some suggest that we should put it on every page. Certainly we need one; as the present Bishop of Durham has said in this context, 'Blessed is he who aims at nothing; for he shall not be disappointed.' A clear aim will affect not only the contents of a sermon, but its structure. First, it will affect the introduction. Obviously, this must be designed to interest people, but it must not be presented as elaborate sugaring leading to the inevitable pill. People quickly see through that method — not least the young for whom it is often used! We have all heard long and brilliant introductions which are only tenuously related to all that follows. If a story or life-situation leads into the message, well and good. But people who regularly attend the Eucharist expect some exposition of what has been read, and if their preacher has a message, they do not need each time to be wheedled into listening. Of course 'The Church bids us on this Sunday. . . ' is deadly; but 'Why did Paul say that?' is not. And in this case, as in so many connected with preaching, *variety* is always to be sought.

The same consideration applies to the illustrations. They are important because they can clinch a point, and because concentration requires light and shade in the sermon. But people have a habit of forgetting sermons and remembering illustrations. This is no bad thing (why otherwise do we find parables in the Gospels?) provided that the illustrations do in fact illustrate what they are meant to illustrate. Laughter ought sometimes to be the response of the congregation, but it is tempting just to raise a laugh for the sake of it.

3

A degree of repetition is effective and important if points are to go home. But it should never be laboured. It is not essential that the conclusion of a sermon should always summarise what has been said before. Sometimes this is useful, but, again it should not be invariable. We have, from the Gospels, good precedent for leaving people with the question 'What do you think?' And it is always essential to stop when you have said all that you want to say.

Preachers who take their scripts into the pulpit — and even those who don't — would be wise to consider the way in which they set out their sermons, and even the paper on which they are written. For many years, I helped train theological students who normally had to write an essay each week. It was difficult to wean them away from an essay-style when they were preparing sermons — especially if those sermons were written on the same sort of paper that they used for their essays. It is salutary for most of us to go through our scripts, chopping up long sentences, reducing subordinate clauses, and trying to remember that people will have *one* opportunity of *listening* to this, not two or three opportunities of reading it. The sermons of Peter Marshall provide an example of how the writing might be set out.

In this brief introduction I am not attempting to summarise what used to involve a course of lectures, or that which can be found in several excellent books on this subject. But I must conclude with one point so obvious that it is often overlooked. This concerns the voice and bearing of the preacher. He may have wrestled long hours in prayer, in reading and in writing. But if he is not actually *heard* because he is inaudible or monotonous — much of his labour is wasted. It's true — sad, maybe, but still true — that very thin material well delivered is more likely to be heard than very profound stuff which is not.

To These Sermons

In the Anglican tradition, the sermon has a setting in worship. It does not dominate the worship, but should arise from the ordered arrangements for that worship, of which the lectionary is one.

Only on the most rare occasions should it be unrelated to the other variable elements in worship — among them, the hymns and the prayers. An appendix to the book offers some suggestions about these things and in particular about hymns — which, while being chosen for their suitability to the points in the liturgy for which they are intended, should be in some way reflective of the theme selected for the sermon. A preacher should therefore be invited to make some suggestions about the hymns to be sung in the service, or, at least, asked for his theme in order that they can be chosen more effectively. Some preachers seem rather coy about this, but it is important in the ordering of the worship. As I have argued in my book *These are the Hymns* (SPCK 1973), the effect of a sermon can be minimised if the next words that the congregation sing have no bearing upon it.

These sermons are for the Christian Year, and are not based exclusively upon the readings for the Sunday Eucharist. Nevertheless, I have born in mind that the Eucharist is, in many parishes, the main occasion of preaching, and in a number of cases, have indicated a variety of ways in which the material might be used.

For *Advent* I have suggested a course. Courses do arouse, and it is to be hoped, hold the interest of the congregations. This is particularly true of our own times when people are accustomed to watch serials on television. A further value of a course in Advent is that it highlights the season, and prevents it from becoming just a prelude to Christmas which tends to begin and end earlier with each year that passes. 'The coming of Christ' is an obvious theme, and I have tried to tackle what we can mean by the phrase 'Christ will come again' which is stated so categorically in the new liturgy. But I have put this into a wider context, and among books that have helped is the small paper-back *Christ Comes In* by Bishop John Robinson.

The broad themes for the Sundays in Advent themselves constitute a possible course for this season. Consonant with them would be an exploration into what is meant by the Kingdom of God; so would be an exposition of the liturgical material provided by the psalms, Benedictus and Magnificat. And, of course, there are still 'The Four Last Things' though they are not precisely suggested by the lectionary.

The main difficulty of preaching at *Christmas* is *when* to do so. Little 'messages' are frequently requested, but in many parishes, the principal gatherings for worship are the Carol Service and the Midnight Eucharist. If the planning of the carol service is flexible, and the Nine Lessons not rigidly adhered to, there is a possibility of a sermon here. Happily sermons at the Midnight Eucharist are now much more common than was once the case. At such, brevity is required, but if the service is well-planned, there is room for more than two minutes from the chancel step. The variety of lessons in the new lectionary give wider scope to the preacher than did the invariable passages from Hebrews and John; and the Lucan Gospel is the basis for the sermon printed here. The sermon for *Epiphany* is intended for the day of that festival; the readings for the following Sunday restore the Baptism of Christ to a more prominent position, but if that is the theme for the Sunday Eucharist, the material here might be used at Evensong, or perhaps for an Epiphany carol service. It is, I think, not true to say that the seasons of Christmas and Epiphany teach their own lessons without benefit of preaching; some of us are more worried about what the religious have done to Christmas than by its so-called secularisation.

For *Lent*, I have provided another course, and this is traditional at this time. It does not fit into the Sunday arrangements, old or new, for this season, but could be used for a week-day course, or in the context of a Bible-study. It is, in any case, assumed that those present will have before them the text of the Psalm to be discussed. In addition to the commentaries, I have found much help in Kenneth Slack's *New Light on Old Songs* as well as the little gold-mine called *The Psalms in Human Life*.

The *Passiontide* sermons were designed for a church which had the 'Preaching of the Cross' for the first two of the 'Three Hours' and the Liturgy for the third — a not uncommon practice at the present time. But they could be used in Lent, or on the evenings of Holy Week. The *Easter* sermon is based upon the 'Easter Anthems' — provided by the New Lectionary as well as the Book of Common Prayer as an integral part of the liturgy of this day.

Sermons for other festivals need no further explanation, but perhaps a word should be said about *Trinity Sunday*. Most people quail before this, and suppose that they must (or should) 'preach on the Trinity'. Few people are capable of tackling the doctrine head-on more than once in every few years, and an alternative starting point (as with the other festivals) is the scriptures from which it has been derived. This is the approach that I suggest here.

The remainder of the book is devoted to sermons for other occasions in the year. Those under the title 'Special Groups' were indeed written for such groups. But they may suggest ideas for Sundays in the regular calendar (e.g. 'Teachers' for the ninth Sunday before Easter, and 'Nurses' for the eighth). The sermon called 'Minorities' was designed for the patronal festival of a church where not too much was known about the patron saint. The 'Special Occasions' are those which occur in most parishes or deaneries. The course called 'Character in Changing Times' was based upon the Mattins lesson (Old Lectionary) for three Sundays after Trinity. It might also be used in a Bible-study. I have been very much helped by the character-studies which appear in the older books of D. W. Cleverley Ford, and by the famous sermon of F. W. Robertson (the nineteenth century preacher who speaks most to me) called 'The Character of Eli'. Of the four individual sermons with which the book concludes, two were written for Evensong (Old Lectionary); but 'Prejudice' is appropriate to Pentecost 16 (New Lectionary), and 'Old and New' is offered as a liturgical tract for the times!

'He must increase and I must decrease' said John the Baptist. The author would rejoice in the decreasing value of these sermons if it meant an increase of the time and trouble that his readers took over their own.

ADVENT

1 The Coming of Christ

Ten years ago, when landings on the moon were all the news, a preacher got up into the pulpit, and delivered what must have been one of the shortest sermons on record. He said simply: 'My friends, we live on a *visited planet*'.

I'm afraid that this sermon will not be quite so short. But it will, I hope, be as simple. For it is concerned to make this same point — we live on a visited planet.

This is Advent Sunday. Our theme is 'The Coming of Christ'. On this theme, the scriptures appointed to be read at this season play so many variations. At one moment, we are on our way to Bethlehem where the Lord comes as a helpless infant; at another, we are at the end of time where he comes to claim the whole universe as his own. We read parables which speak of the immediacy of judgement as we go about our daily concerns, and we are shown great tapestries which depict the grand assize that is to be held over the whole of human history. Bishop John Robinson once wrote, 'What the four weeks of the Advent season do is, as it were, to give us a series of "stills" from a continuous film, flashing upon the screen Sunday by Sunday different moments in Christ's constant coming.'

We need to look at those stills. We need time to do so. We need the season of Advent. People often moan about the commercialisation of Christmas, and certainly it seems to start a bit earlier with every year that passes. In some churches there is 'agro' about the date of the carol service, and whether or not carols should be sung at all before Christmas Eve. All this sounds a niggling and ecclesiastical sort of controversy — when the rest of the world is eating Christmas dinners at office parties and singing Christmas carols in school concerts throughout the whole of December. But what the sticklers are trying to do is to preserve not only Advent but Christmas itself. You miss a great deal of what Christmas is about if you miss what Advent has to say. The Christian message does not begin and end with St Luke 2 — which may have been something of an after-thought to that Gospel anyway. In one church they had a lovely custom when 24 December happened to fall on a Sunday. The Parish Communion was celebrated in the bare church, with the purple hangings and the last of the Advent hymns. Then, after coffee, the whole congregation set to, and decorated the place for Christmas. It was probably less professional and less perfect than it might have been if a group of trained ladies had done it a few days earlier. But everyone enjoyed Christmas because they had kept Advent.

However the preacher must substantiate what he is saying. Christmas needs to be put into context if it is to be properly understood. And the context is this — that God is always visiting and redeeming his people. This is the biblical picture. This is the tradition of Christianity, and its parent Judaism. These traditions are always seeing God as involved with men and women. They don't speculate much about God in himself. They can't envisage a God who is all alone. Maybe they've missed out on something here, maybe this is something which other religions could teach us. But the biblical account is all about a God who is concerned with us. The first pages of the Bible show the picture of the Garden of Eden, and the Lord asking Adam 'Where art thou?' And almost its last words are 'Yes, I am coming soon.' Between these two points lie the whole story of the divine involvement with humanity. We see a God quaintly described as one who 'rises up early' to send the prophets. We see one who communicates with us through what might seem the bounties of nature or the ironies of fate, we see one who speaks through dreams and messengers. Here is one who leads Abraham into new territory, who notices Ruth because of her simple devotion, who spots Jeremiah as a man who will proclaim the message because he feels it for himself. This is the context of Christmas and the coming of Christ — a God who cares so much for his people, who must come both in judgement and mercy because he knows what they can be.

The story does not end with Christmas. Nor does it end with Easter for that matter. We have seen that the readings for this season take us at one moment into the past, at another into the future, and at yet another point as unmistakably to the present. Advent is about all three. Advent is not just a preparation for the end of time — as some of our forefathers supposed. It is not just a prelude to the celebration of Bethlehem — as is often popularly thought. And it is not just an alerting of ourselves to present judgement — as many scholars of this century have urged. It is all three. All three belong together, but because we can only take in so much at a time, we are going to consider them separately on the Sundays in Advent: the Christ who *came*, the Christ who *comes*, and the Christ who *will* come. Four Sundays are not too many for this theme. We need Advent.

But, much more than that, we need to know of a God who is made real to us because he is always coming to us. There is a special atmosphere about this Sunday. Maybe it's the nearness of Christmas; or the fact that it has been traditionally the beginning of a new Christian Year; or even the great hymns of this season. But through it all there is the reality of a God longing to make himself known to hearts that wait for him.

ADVENT

2 The Christ who came

The life of Jesus is a best-seller. Books about him are assured of a market — especially if written by laymen! Television series like 'Jesus of Nazareth' have an enormous viewing public. You can't fail to be gripped by the story. But as you read it or watch it, there are nagging doubts — Is it true? How much of it really happened?

If there were no collection of books called the New Testament, we should still know that a man called Jesus lived and was crucified at this time in history. But we should not know much more. We are dependent, in the main, on the four Gospels. And most people know something of their story — that there was a long gap between the death of Jesus and the first recorded accounts of his life, that there weren't reporters of newspapers to carry the story. And those who have been taught something about the Gospels in recent years know more — that they seem to

11

be collections of material put together in the early Church, arranged probably for its worship, designed not as biographies but as proclamations of Jesus as the Messiah, passed on by word of mouth. There is plenty of room for mistakes in this process, for getting things wrong, for getting them out of focus. You see how this can happen by comparing certain incidents, seeing how they are differently treated in different Gospels. You can imagine the process.

So the question arises — how far can we trust these documents? How can we know that Jesus did and said things he is supposed to have done and said? I think we must be quite honest here and admit that we can't — that events may well have been altered in the telling. At the same time, there is no ground for the complete scepticism that sometimes seems to be the alternative. Here are two reasons.

First, what has almost become fiction can have its basis in fact. Take one famous story in the Gospels — the stilling of the storm on the sea of Galilee. Scholars tell us that this was used in the early Church as a way of illustrating God's care for his people — his Church — that they can have peace even in the storms that surround them. This is a valuable way of interpreting the story, and it is one which we still use when we sing verses like:

> See round thy ark the hungry billows curling
> See how thy foes their banners are unfurling;
> Lord, while their darts envenomed they are hurling,
> Thou canst preserve us.

But if you go to Israel, you can still make the crossing of the sea from Tiberias. You can experience the suddenness of the storm where the waters had recently been so placid — and you can find no earthly reason why such an incident could not have taken place. Things which have been altered, interpreted, maybe sometimes misunderstood, can still have happened.

Secondly, it seems to have been common at the time of Jesus for disciples of various sects to learn word for word the sayings of their teacher. Discoveries at the Dead Sea have very much increased our knowledge of such sects. Some of the stories about

Jesus and the sayings of Jesus, even though they depended on oral transmission, may well have been passed on with the greatest care. Because the Christian community was so careful to preserve the tradition that Jesus said 'Do this in remembrance of me' there is very strong reason to believe that he did!

So in these Gospels, with all their discrepancies, with all allowance for a margin of error, we have a reliable account of what Jesus was like. Of course it is incomplete. But, then, it must be so. For in the person of Jesus himself, there is that which is mysterious. Neither his family nor his friends understood him completely. If you think you completely understand any human being, you're mistaken. A measure of mystery is part of the dignity of being human at all; it must be no less true of him who is declared to stand in unique relationship to God himself.

The fact is that we know enough — not enough perhaps, for curiosity, but enough for faith. The Gospels were written to evoke faith, and they exist to evoke faith today. The Christ who spoke in them is still the Christ who speaks to us. When *we* are careful and troubled about many things, he still tells us that one thing is needful; when *we* seem paralysed by the circumstances of life and what we have made of them, he still tells us that our sins are forgiven, and that we must rise and walk. When *we* are being a bit too clever, we are shown pictures in which we hear the words 'Go and do as he did.'

Our subject is 'the Christ who came' but inevitably we have moved on to 'the Christ who comes'. Our study of Christ in the Gospels — indeed of the whole Bible, for which we give thanks on this Sunday — is not just an academic matter. Of course we want to know, so far as we can, what it all was like. We must take that trouble if we are to understand anything about him at all. But our study of the Christ who came is primarily in order to know the Christ who comes. In what may have been the original ending of St John's Gospel, the evangelist says, 'There were indeed many other signs that Jesus performed in the presence of his disciples, which are not recorded in this book. Those here written have been recorded in order that you may come to believe that Jesus is the Christ, the Son of God, and that through this faith, you may possess life by his Name.'

13

ADVENT

3 The Christ who comes

Last Sunday we thought of the Christ who came. And inevitably we began to think of the Christ who comes. We saw that our study of the Gospels can never be simply of academic interest. We ask what Jesus was like and what sort of things he said in order to understand what he *is* like and what sort of things he *is* saying. When Jesus 'went away' from his disciples, it was in order that he might be more fully with them. 'Where two or three are gathered together in my name, there am I in the midst of them' is one of his recorded sayings. And although there has long been doubt about the date of the last verses in St Matthew's Gospel, there is no doubt that the words 'Be assured, I am with you always, to the end of time' represent the conviction of the early Church.

But in what sense is he 'with us'? And how does he come? We have already begun to find part of the answer to those questions. He is 'with us' in all that is covered by the old phrase 'the means of grace'. One of these, as we have seen, is to be found in the scriptures — which we must approach with intelligence as well as imagination. Another is prayer — in all its forms, which include listening and seeking as well as asking and thanking. Another is the sacrament of Holy Communion, where the key word 'remembrance' suggests bringing into the present what happened in the past. In all these ways, he comes to arouse us and to encourage us, to check us and to strengthen us.

It has been noted that in the Gospels not too many people got a personal, private interview with Jesus, but that more often he was to be seen only in the company of his friends. So the activities that we have mentioned are corporate as well as individual. And that is where the Church comes in. Leave aside for a moment its structures and its assemblies, and think of it as it is meant to be — a company of Jesus' disciples. He comes as people meet together. The Scriptures can be illuminated for us as members of a group share their insights and questions, or as one, fully trained and authorised, seeks to interpret their meaning. And our Church has always insisted that there cannot be a Eucharist unless there are communicants — Christ comes not only when the elements are consecrated, but when they are divided and shared.

But public worship and private prayer are not invariably vibrant. There are many times when we don't feel like either; there are many times when the first is dull, and the second seems meaningless. Sometimes this is our fault, and sometimes it isn't. There will always be a certain ebb and flow in the spiritual life. All sorts of things can be said individually about it, but in general, perhaps the most helpful is that we must come to these things *expecting* that through them Christ will come to us.

We have been thinking of ways in which we have been taught to look for the presence of Christ. But he comes to us not only in expected ways, but in unexpected. And in fact, from the earliest days, people have been told that he will come in the unexpected, and have often conveniently forgotten the possibility. The great parables which we read at this season often speak of common-place situations, in which people are being judged by their response. One of these is the story of the sheep and goats. You recall the perplexity of the question, 'Lord, when was it that we saw you hungry and fed you, or thirsty and gave you drink, a stranger and took you home, or naked and clothed you?'

There was a certain un-self-consciousness about those who acted in this way, as well as insensitivity about those who didn't. But years of familiarity with this story cannot dull its impact — the incredible fact that the Lord of Glory, the Perfect Man comes to us still in the abject and the wretched; and that as we seek to share our lives and our goods with the poor, we are actually ministering to him.

So he comes to us — unexpectedly and often inconveniently — through those who need our help. But he comes as well through those who give it to us. A great preacher of yesterday, Dr Leslie Weatherhead, recalled visiting a young woman who had lost her husband after three months of marriage. Her mother was trying to comfort her. The young woman asked Weatherhead 'You preached once on the Everlasting Arms: where are they now?' And after a time, he pointed to the arms of the *mother*. Christ comes to us through the people, the very ordinary people, who do things for us.

Many of the hymns of Advent sing of wakefulness, watchfulness, being on the alert. Many of them were devised with the 'second coming' in mind. Next week we shall try to see what we can mean by that. But we can be ready for Christ's final coming only if we are ready for his coming now. Around us in Advent is a feeling of expectancy — which affects us all despite the crowds and the shopping and our saying that we shall be glad when it's over! But Christian expectancy is not only of Christmas, but of Christ. And what we are told to do at this time is to look for every sign of his coming. This can revive our worship and our prayers — and, what is even more important, help us to recognise and welcome him, wherever he is in his world.

ADVENT

4 The Christ who will come

The first Christians thought that Christ would soon come again. They thought of that in a literal sense, and not in the way we were thinking last week. But in every century, there have been those who thought in that literal way. At the end of the second century, a priest called Montanus claimed special revelation and led his followers to a remote village in the waste of Phrygia where they awaited the coming of the new Jerusalem. It did not come; so they built an earthly city instead, and formed a sect known as Montanism.

There are people in this century who will tell you that Christ is coming again. You find them in small sects, but you find them in the larger churches as well. The Series 3 Communion service contains the phrase in the Thanksgiving itself: 'Christ will come again' and it has remained there despite many revisions. But most Christians have tended to ignore this phrase — which we also have in the Creeds — or else to disbelieve it. They have ignored it because century has followed century since these beliefs were commonly held; and they have disbelieved it because the pictures drawn in the New Testament seem incredible.

16

But it is not enough to dismiss what we do not understand or to ignore what we find unpalatable. Leave aside the pretensions of those who claim to know when the Lord will come, and what will be the manner of his coming. Leave aside those who have used the New Testament as though it were *Old Moore's Almanack*, and have not bothered to understand its background. We must still give attention to a belief strongly held by the first Christians, and held at various times, and with varying degrees of intensity, during the centuries that follow. We must ask whether the idea that Christ will come again has any meaning for us now.

In order to find the answer, we must look at the background of those parts of the Gospels that seem to predict a literal return of Jesus. They are not original to Christianity. This vivid language — lurid language sometimes — comes from the centuries that immediately preceded Christ, and had become an almost conventional way in which to describe the reality of God's deliverance and his triumph. We must notice also that the first Christians believed that God had intervened in human history through Jesus, and that although the kingdom had yet to be fulfilled, it had in fact come. In *The Christian Hope*, J.E. Fison, the last Bishop of Salisbury wrote:

> When we turn to the New Testament we see that the radical intellectual problem was how to express at one and the same time the conviction that in Christ the end had arrived, and also that in some equally vivid way, it was to be imminently expected in the future. But what is intellectually obscure and incomprehensible for logical reasons becomes mystically clear and unmistakable in the relationship of love, for whereas in logic if you possess something it is unreasonable to go on hoping for it, in love that is exactly what you must do. The extent of your present possession is the measure of your future expectation.

The Christ who was crucified, risen and ascended is the One whose triumph over all things must ultimately be declared and seen. This is the truth to which the Christian faith bears witness when it uses phrases like 'Christ will come again'. Perhaps the phrase could be replaced by something less misleading. The organisation called the Modern Churchmen's Union challenged the Liturgical Commission to do just this during the discussions about how the Thanksgiving in Series 3 might be revised. But it remains a fundamental conviction that the purposes of God must be fulfilled. That is in itself a rather prosaic phrase, and maybe we need poetry and art to reveal what prose cannot. For in speaking of these things, we move outside our normal thinking in terms of time and space; and that is what we get when the Gospels paint, as it were, huge tapestries, which reveal the victory of God over everything that opposes his will.

Sometimes those pictures have struck terror and often they have been meant to do so. But the Christ who will come is not different from the Christ who came, and the Christ who comes to us now. He is, again to use the language of symbolism, the Christ who still bears the prints of the wounds in his hands and his feet, the Christ who still suffers for his people — as love must suffer until it has won the beloved.

The future of this world has exercised many of our best minds during the years that have followed the second World War. At one time, the main threat to civilisation seemed to lie in nuclear explosion, and it is a threat that has by no means been removed from us. Then we have had the repeated warnings about the using up of the earth's resources, so that life becomes hardly worth living (even if it is possible to live it) for the human race. No scientific prognosis for our future seems very promising.

And there are those who look forward to the Christmas break, and wonder why the sermon need be so depressing. The Christian faith offers more than temporary jollity, or an anaesthetic against this world's pain. It offers the assurance that the love, which in our better moments, we prize most is that which matters most — that beyond our anxieties and fears is the God whose nature was disclosed in Christ — that the One who came is the One who will come. And with that knowledge comes confidence, peace and joy.

CHRISTMAS

We can't imagine Christmas without shepherds. They stand around the crib, and look out at us from Christmas cards. They add to the romance and charm of the scene. We know how important they were to the civilisation described in the Bible, and therefore it is not surprising that St Luke should mention them in his account of Christ's birth.

But when you write your Christmas letters (or the ones you promise to write after Christmas!) you're not short of news for those you love. There are thoughts you would like to share with them, incidents that you know would amuse them. But time and paper mean that you must make a selection. So it was with the Gospel-writers. There may have been many traditions about the birth of Jesus. Luke has good reasons for choosing what he did, and we must pay careful attention to his selection.

The mention of shepherds is not accidental or haphazard, nor is it intended to provide pictureque detail. For, in the first place Jesus came of shepherd-stock. Israel's greatest and most glamorous king was a shepherd boy, and Luke is careful to tell us that Jesus belonged to the house of David. The biblical writers are deeply interested in heredity, in a man's ante-natal story. The one born in a manger had a royal pedigree, and he was to occupy the throne of David. But the house of David had fallen on evil days. Disaster and defeat had overtaken the kings of Israel and Judah and — according to the Old Testament writers — they richly deserved it. Now the course of things would be changed again. All that people had hoped for in David and his successors would be fulfilled — and much more.

Secondly, Jesus received the adoration of the shepherds. They were the first to greet Him. Much is made of the simplicity or humility of the shepherds, and this can be misunderstood. They were certainly not the lowest of the low. They were skilled, resourceful, intelligent people — they had to be to do their work effectively. When David slung stones at Goliath, he had probably learned the art because he was a shepherd, and knew how to ward off attacks from wild beasts. But the shepherd was a nomad; his work didn't give him opportunity to participate in the customs of his people — like going to synagogue. We learn from ancient writers that, for this reason, shepherds tended to be despised by orthodox religious people of the day. Yet they prefigure the multitude of ordinary people who have been attracted by Jesus. Others were to follow in St Luke's Gospel — like Simeon and Anna who watched and waited in the Temple. But the *first* worshippers were the shepherds.

Thirdly, Jesus was to be one of them. In St John's Gospel, he is described as the Good Shepherd, but here in Luke he tells the parable of the sheep that was lost and the shepherd who went after it. The idea of Jesus as the Shepherd persists in the New Testament and in Christian devotion based upon it — for he is the One who searches for his sheep, who cares for them, and leads them to pasture. Again the word 'shepherd' in ancient Israel was often used of those whose business it was to look after the spiritual needs of the people; and we certainly find denunciation of the false shepherds who sought only their own welfare and were not concerned with that of the people they were appointed to serve. But all that is best in the shepherd's job is to be seen in the Good Shepherd who ultimately gave his life for the sheep.

This sermon has been about Jesus, and this is surely appropriate on his birthday. But his coming to us means identification with us, and so it is that the things of which we have been thinking have a bearing upon ourselves. So let's look at them again.

First, Jesus is descended from the shepherd-king. But that king's descendants had been unworthy of the trust put upon them, and Jesus' own pedigree included some less creditable characters. Whatever has happened to our lives, whatever has distorted and spoilt them can be put right. Heredity, environment and circumstance do not have the last word about our destiny. Jesus the Saviour is born; and he can save and redeem us — however much life's blows or our own sins seem to have dragged us down.

And then the shepherds were the first to welcome him. He accepts us as we are. Indeed we cannot be other than we are when we stand before the crib and the cross. A parson's wife said the other day that when she joined the wives' group in her husband's theological college, she always felt inferior — the others seemed so much more devout and gifted than herself. Have you ever felt like that in a Christian group? Jesus does not want us to be complacent, but equally he doesn't want us to feel inferior. The first worshippers were the ordinary people — not the church leaders or the civic leaders, nor the particularly religious, but the shepherds. And he calls us to be his friends.

Thirdly, he wants us to share in his pastoral work. He invites us to search, to care and sometimes to lead those whom he loves in this world. He asks us to do this as we go about our normal life. It was to Peter — who denied him — that he said 'Feed my sheep, tend my lambs'. It is our hands, our feet, our lips that he must now use.

The shepherds returned rejoicing and praising God. They are described in one of the greatest Christmas hymns as 'The first apostles of his infant fame.' We can be their successors. You know that the praise of God involves not only the words of our lips, but the actions of our lives. So may the joy of Christ be with you — and flow out from you.

EPIPHANY

We should like to stay with Christmas, but we *must* go on to Epiphany. Perhaps you are rather relieved. When Christmas decorations go up in the streets in October, and carols blare out at the end of November, then it's time to move on.

Yet I think the Church often wants to stay with Christmas. The Christmas story is the story of the in-group — the holy family, the shepherds, even the innkeeper, all belong to the same race, all share the same background. Epiphany brings strangers into the story. They are people of different customs, maybe people of different colour. Epiphany breaks into the cosiness of Christmas. Epiphany makes us face up to the realities of the world. I say that the Church often wants to stay with Christmas, because it's often afraid of Epiphany. The fellowship of our churches is a great deal warmer, and their atmosphere more frank and honest than was the case even a quarter of a century ago; but the price for all this is that we tend to be inward looking, satisfied with a good average number of communicants. The 'explanation' of the parable of wheat and tares begins, 'The field is the world'; we often make the field the Church.

Epiphany is the meeting point between Christ and the world. The strangers 'from Persian lands afar' have always been seen as the first Gentile worshippers of Christ. They symbolise the truth that Christ is not tied to one sort of culture or one period of history, but that he is for all men and women. He is the Light of the World; and, as Evelyn Underhill once said, that does not mean the sanctuary lamp in our favourite church.

All this means that the mission of the Church is an indispensable part of the existence of the Church. Christ is the Light who enlightens the darkness of this world. A few years ago Jehovah's Witnesses were accustomed to start a conversation with the words, 'Don't you think the world is in a terrible state?' You could not say anything but 'Yes'. It needs no preacher to demonstrate the blackness of things. The media do it for us most effectively. The evils of the world and the sins of human beings are more newsworthy than the goodness of the world and the virtues of human beings. Greed and selfishness, ignorance and indifference, cruelty and oppression — of all these we have daily instances. We can certainly see the difference that the Christian Gospel could make — love where there is hate, forgiveness instead of revenge, acceptance in the place of rejection. These things could change our world. There can be no question about the 'relevance' of Christianity. Jesus Christ could still bring light to a world of darkness.

This is set out in the Epiphany story. The Scriptures of the Old Testament point forward to this Light; those of the New Testament declare that it has dawned. Both the Acts of the Apostles and the subsequent history of the Church show that Christ has become Lord to people of many cultures, many races. The strangers at the crib were indeed the first fruits of a great harvest.

But is there another side to the Epiphany story? Christianity has everything to offer to the world; has the world anything to offer in return? There are hints that it has. When the Magi came to Bethlehem, they offered gifts to the Child. Now there is more than one interpretation of this. The word 'magi' can mean 'wise men' or it can mean 'magicians'. Wise men may have presented gifts befitting Christ — and the Christian tradition has dwelt lovingly and imaginatively on their significance. But magicians may have cast down at his feet the tools of a trade that they now despised. Perhaps both interpretations now have something to say to us. When people come to Christ, there are things they must give up, things they used to prize, things that the world prizes. Among them are the lust for power, the lust for money or the lust for ease. But maybe they also have something to give. Jesus once told his disciples that they could learn a few things from a dishonest bailiff. And on many occasions, he pointed out the truths of the kingdom by noticing the way in which the world went about its business.

What then, has this aspect of the Epiphany story to say to us about mission? It tells us that convictions must be held with humility. Never must Christians give the impression that they have a monopoly of truth or wisdom, and most certainly not of virtue. A few years ago we often heard the cliché 'the world sets the agenda' and that means that the Christian Gospel must be addressed to the world as it is, not to what we think it is, or what we would like it to be. It means moreover, as leaders of our missionary societies have long been telling us, that we do not merely 'take Christ' to other people, but look for him among them, and help them to see him there as well. How often we are put to shame when we find in entirely secular institutions a compassion and concern that exceed that of many churches. We ought to react in penitence because it is less obvious among us, but also to rejoice that it is found among them.

Giving and receiving go together. Love, so far as we understand it at all, involves mutuality. In Steinbeck's *East of Eden* the father's great defect is that he never *wants* anything from the 'difficult' son. God does want our love, our gifts whatever they may be; why else would we hear parables of a father who watched for a prodigal son, or a shepherd who left ninety-nine in search of one? For he who has everything to give is yet incomplete without the response of his children.

ASH WEDNESDAY

Gospel. St Matthew 6. 16–21

We all understand the negative side of these verses. We know that they were directed against those who were ostentatious in their religious practices, and we can see how they may be applied today. But let's look at the positive side of this passage, and so take as our text St Matthew 6.17,18.

'When you fast, anoint your head and wash your face, so that men may not see that you are fasting, but only your Father, who is in the secret place; and your Father who sees in secret will give you your reward.'

In this chapter, Jesus assumes that his disciples will continue the religious customs practised by devout Jews in his day. These included prayer, fasting and acts of charity, and he has the same sort of thing to say about all three. There is to be a place in the Christian life for discipline and self-denial, and we have come to that season of the year when this part of our calling is brought home to us. In these verses we are told how it should be undertaken. Implied in it are three things which are closely related, but which we will take separately.

First of all, fasting, like prayer and acts of charity, is to be *in secret*. I don't think this precludes group activity. Our generation has rightly reacted against the wrong kind of individualism. In the Roman Catholic Church, a corporate act of penitence followed by absolution sometimes replaces the confessional. Many Evangelicals find it more profitable to read the Bible with a group than on their own. Some people go in for a sponsored slim during Lent, and they have the support and help of others who are doing the same thing — which is the principle on which Weight-

Watchers or Alcoholics Anonymous work. But whether we undertake discipline in groups or as individuals, it is important that we do not draw attention to ourselves, that we do not force our ideas upon other people, that we do not so parade our fasting as to make others uncomfortable. If we do, then we have our reward. And it is a cheap one.

That brings us to the second point — that our fasting must be *sincere*. In *The Cost of Discipleship* Dietrich Bonhoeffer wrote, 'Strict exercise of self-control is an essential part of the Christian life. Customs of fasting have only one purpose — to make the disciples more ready and cheerful to accomplish those things which God would have done.'

Fasting may be good for us. Losing weight may be good for us. But Lent does not exist for the improvement of our figures. What we save on ourselves can be given to those who need it. The great Anglican divine, Jeremy Taylor, combined practical maxims on the devotional life with a superb English style and not a little humour. And he wrote on this theme, 'A man must not, when he mourns in his fast, be merry in his sport; weep at dinner and laugh all day after; have silence in his kitchen, and music in his chamber; judge the stomach, and feast the other senses.'

Our discipline must build us up, and make us better instruments of God's purposes.

So, thirdly, our fastings must be *positive*. Lent comes with lengthening days, and ought, in every sense to be a looking towards the light. The origins of this season lie, at least partly, in the period when candidates were undergoing their final preparation for baptism, which took place at Easter. In many parishes, there has been revived the custom of renewing baptismal vows on Easter Eve, and those vows remind us that we have passed from darkness to light. As we think of this, so the season becomes one in which we put ourselves to school again, being willing to explore more deeply the things of Christ, and to carry out more resolutely the will of Christ. So be sure that whatever you 'give up' during Lent, you also 'take on' some corresponding thing — something to increase your understanding and devotion, something to increase your service and effectiveness.

And all this brings us to what is meant by 'reward' in this context. As used in this passage it does not refer to what we may expect to receive at the end of time — but to the present spiritual benefits that will come if our fasting, like our prayer and acts of charity are undertaken in the right spirit: that is, secretly, sincerely, and positively.

LENT

INSIGHTS FROM THE PSALMS

1 Realism — Psalm 90

It is good for preachers to hear sermons — and sometimes to read them. I want to tell you about one printed sermon that recently changed some of my attitudes and practice.

The preacher was Bernard Manning, Cambridge historian and Free Churchman, whose main work was done between the wars. One authority on preaching has put Manning alongside C. S. Lewis as outstanding examples of distinguished lay preaching in this century. The sermon was entitled 'The Burial of the Dead' and in the course of it, Manning pleaded for the retention of Psalm 90 in the Burial Service appointed in the Prayer Book (and indeed, in the new services). Now, like many clergy, I had commonly used Psalm 23 at funerals, thinking that the service ought to give comfort and hope from start to finish.

Psalm 90 hardly does that. It is a lament on the brevity of life. As such, it strikes a note of realism. In the last few years, we have been told many times and by many sorts of people that we must not sweep death under the carpet. At some funerals, there is a studied attempt to ignore the fact of death. When it comes to the hymns people choose, 'For all the saints' which, as the verses go on, makes fairly large assumptions about the departed, or even 'Praise my soul, the king of heaven' which has nothing whatever to do with the occasion, but is generally considered to be cheerful!

Yet the recognition of our mortality, and our facing up to its sorrow can have a carthartic effect upon us. And it can be a necessary prelude to the hearing of the Gospel — traditionally on this occasion declared in 1 Corinthians 15.

Some people say that they are not afraid of death. Rare souls like St Francis can welcome 'Kind and gentle Sister Death,' but for most of us, a surer note is struck in *Measure for Measure*:

> The weariest and most loathed wordly life
> That age, ache, penury and imprisonment
> Can lay on Nature, is a paradise
> To what we fear of death.

If Christian worship is to correspond to all that we are, there is room for lament as well as exultation, for question as well as for affirmation. The Psalms are notable for the variety of human emotions which they express, and we would be impoverished if we lost that variety. This is not to say that all the psalms are suitable for regular public worship. But when you turn out a cupboard, you sometimes come across forgotten objects that can have a new usefulness. So it is with psalms that are not so well-known, not so often used. Perhaps Psalm 90 is one of them.

I want you to notice four things about it. First, it opens with a song of praise and wonder at the eternity of God. This occupies the psalmist for the first two verses. He thinks of God's majesty before he goes on to man's misery. We are conscious of the brevity of our life, because we have some inkling of eternity. The Greek poets called us the 'mortals' by contrast with the gods whom they believed to be immortal. The second theme of the Psalm is contained in verses 3 to 11. This is the lament on the transience of life, the pathos of age, the inevitability of death, and the divine wrath which must be the result of the clash between man's arrogance and God's goodness. On some of these themes we have already touched. Now in verse 12 we have a further reflection. It is a brief recognition of the importance of life. The psalmist does not encourage us to enjoy our own melancholy, but to value and appreciate what we have here and now. John Newton, the eighteenth-century Evangelical and hymn-writer lived in an age which revelled in death-bed scenes. Newton said once 'Tell me not how a man died, but how he lived.' This the psalmist encourages in the third theme. The fourth is brought out in the final verses: 13–17, which are of hope. The future as well as the past is the hands of God. And he is a God of mercy.

That is as far as the psalmist can take us. There is, thank God, far more to our faith than this. But we need the insight that he has to offer. So we shall soon sing the metrical version which is, in my judgement, even finer than Coverdale's prose. I wish we could sing it with the original opening 'Our God, our help in ages past' which makes all the difference to the hymn; but the substitution might cause confusion at the moment, so we must wait for a better hymn-book! The hymn is indelibly associated with Remembrance Sunday — for which it is appropriate enough. But as you sing it today, try to rid your mind of bugles and poppies and concentrate on the great monolithic Anglo-Saxon words. Remember that you are singing of the sovereignty of God, the brevity of life, the importance of this present moment, and our hope for the future.

The mood of our worship will then change — as it must do. For we worship him who came to break the vicious circle of death and despair. So is this all a bit of make-believe? Are you being asked to be miserable in order to enjoy the happy ending of the story? By no means. For we walk by faith, not by sight. And it is only as we see ourselves as we are in our own sight that we can understand what we are in the sight of God. And then it is that we can hear his word of promise to us.

LENT

INSIGHTS FROM THE PSALMS

2 Opportunity — Psalm 49

You may know the story of the very rich woman who, despite the fact that she was so very rich, managed to get to Heaven. But she was rather disappointed with what she found there. She was not allocated one of the 'many mansions', but was sent instead to what was not much more than a hovel. So she sought out Peter to complain. And Peter said 'But, madam, we did the best we could with the materials that you sent up.'

Today's Psalm is not saying that, but it is saying something very like it. I doubt if Psalm 49 is anyone's favourite. I doubt if it ever has been. Matthew Arnold quotes it rather wryly, but it is not one of the psalms that have been quoted widely in Christian history. It is what is sometimes called a 'wisdom' Psalm; it isn't a shout of praise, or a song of lament, but is concerned instead with admonition. In verses 1–4, the singer addresses the world — high and low, rich and poor. His ear strains to hear the divine voices; and the riddle which he seems to hear, that he declares with music. He is concerned about the tyranny of the rich, but he points out that riches cannot bring immortality either for ourselves or our brother. Verse 12, echoed in verse 20 is rendered in the *Psalms: A New Translation for Worship* as:

A rich man without understanding
Is like the beasts that perish

Verse 13 becomes:

This is the lot of the foolish:
The end of those who are pleased with their own words

The following verse describes the fate of those who trust in their own success, and then verse 15 has one of those hints at immortality that we find scattered about in the Psalter. Then the remainder of the psalm returns to its central theme — Be not afraid, though one be made rich.

Besides the hint of resurrection in verse 15, the Psalm points forward in some interesting ways to the New Testament. As we read it, we are reminded of the story of Dives and Lazarus, or of the parable of the rich fool who built barns to store his produce, but died before he could live comfortably. And the reference to no man being able to ransom his brother reminds us of that famous verse in the Gospels where the Son of Man gives his life as a ransom for many.

This Psalm deals again with the inevitability of death. We noticed when we studied Psalm 90 that this thought is not meant to let us indulge in morbidity; and we noted the striking verse:

So teach us to number our days
that we may apply our hearts unto wisdom.

When the psalmists speak of the brevity of life, it is to tell us to make the most of its opportunities. This Psalm does so rather negatively. But let's look at that negative side.

The writer does what wise men of many faiths have done. He tells us not to rely too much on things like riches, success or other people's praise. We can take none of these things with us. It's almost a truism, yet it is one that we persistently neglect. When we go on adding to our possessions, it is they who begin to possess us. In his book, *God and the Rich Society* Denys Munby wrote, 'The evils of riches, to the Christian, are the evils of distraction (the distraction that keeps men from thinking about God), the evils of a false dependence on the created order, and a would-be security that fails to take account of the inevitable fragility of human destiny on this earth.'

From this consideration come two corollaries. First, we are not to be envious of those better-placed than ourselves. Envy is one of the traditional seven deadly sins, and it is deadly because it can destroy our peace of mind and poison our relationships with others. Secondly, we are not to be too obsequious towards the rich, the powerful or the successful. Ever since Christianity became an established religion, there has been the danger of accepting this world's standards, and absorbing this world's values. Every day, in traditional Anglican Evensong, come the words:

He hath put down the mighty from their seat:
And hath exalted the humble and meek.

but Anglicans have probably not been quite alone in making pretty sure that the mighty were duly ushered to their seat! Yet

The boast of heraldry, the pomp of power,
And all that beauty, all that wealth e'er gave

30

Await alike th' inevitable hour.
The paths of glory lead but to the grave.

It has been said that it is always the rich who preach content-
ment to the poor, but the psalmist is addressing rich and poor
alike. He has to leave it to others to expound what is worthwhile,
what are the treasures of heaven, how we can use the opportunities of life. A group called the Sheldon Theatre Group showed
God as a store-keeper, saying that although all his wares were
free, nobody wanted those that were most valuable. Of such
things Old and New Testaments are full. And they are expressed
in a simple verse by William Blake:

The countless gold of a merry heart,
The rubies and pearls of a loving eye,
The indolent never can bring to the mart,
Nor the cunning hoard up in his treasury.

The present is vital; life never lacks opportunity. The psalmist
warns us not to go down dead ends. But the Gospel tells us to take
those roads that lead to life.

LENT

INSIGHTS FROM THE PSALMS

3 Remorse — Psalm 51

In 'quires and places where they sing' the congregation is often
unusually large on Ash Wednesday. This is not only because
people want to make a good start to Lent, but because the anthem
is commonly the *Miserere* by Allegri. This is one of the most
popular pieces of church music; it has found its way to many
records; it crops up regularly on 'Your Hundred Best Tunes.'

It is the music that makes the words known in our century. But
the Psalm is one of the most influential in Christian history. It was
used constantly in the worship of the medieval Church, and has
been an inspiration to theologians of many traditions. No one can
estimate what it has meant in the lives of individuals. In the

troubled era of the Reformation, both Sir Thomas More and Lady Jane Grey went to the scaffold with these words.

It offers insight on remorse — on the nagging sense of failure which affects so many of us, on the regret we feel because we have missed opportunities that life gave us, on the wounds inflicted on our pride when we remember what we have done to other people, and what a poor showing we have made of ourselves.

The main insight of the Psalm is that it takes us straight to the root of our trouble. It tells us that we have sinned against a holy God. 'Against thee only have I sinned: and done this evil in thy sight.' Maybe we are much more worried about our sins against other people — because, as we have seen, they affect our pride. Perhaps we can see that we sometimes sin against ourselves. But all these things belong together, because we belong to God. The psalmist affirms that standards are more than relative, that 'pure universal Love' is at the centre of all things, and that our sins against others are part of something bigger — our sin against God.

So the psalmist goes on to explore the depth of sin. 'Behold, I was shapen in wickedness: and in sin hath my mother conceived me'. The verse has been taken to mean total depravity, and used to degrade human sexuality. But, in fact, the psalmist is saying something quite modern. As one commentator puts it, 'Original sin is theological terminology for the same facts which science gathers together under the name of "heredity".' There is a distinction in the Bible between 'sin' and 'sins'. When writers like St Paul refer to the former, they mean a disposition to evil. We have within us an innate waywardness which enthrones self where only God should reign. Now of course we would know nothing of 'sin' without 'sins'. But the second is a symptom, and the first the disease. The psalmist knows that he has need of more than palliatives.

This brings us not only to God's willingness to forgive, but to his power to cleanse. 'Thou shalt purge me with hyssop and I shall be clean.' Hyssop was used ritually, but it was a plant known for its healing properties. Alexander Fleming's biographer finds in this verse the first known reference to penicillin. What that discovery has done for the bodies of men, the grace of God can do for his whole being. It can make us what he meant us to be. Whenever we confess our sins and remember God's forgiveness, we ought also to affirm his power to heal. Many Christians find the reality of this through the confessional. But there are other ways of knowing it. In his classic *Private House of Prayer* the late Dr. Leslie Weatherhead had a section called 'Positive affirmation and reception'. In such prayer, we do not ask God to heal, but we affirm that he is doing so. We could turn the verse to 'You are purging me with hyssop, and making me clean.' This is a process, like a course of penicillin. And our willingness to allow God's gracious activity in us means that we can grow — to the stature for which we are intended.

The realisation of this is the cause of the greatest joy we can know on earth, and it is the inspiration of Christian hymns of every generation. The Prayer Book translation of our Psalm has the words:

Thou shalt make me hear of joy and gladness:
that the bones which thou hast broken may rejoice.

But a Hebrew scholar has described as 'woefully inadequate' Coverdale's translation of verse 12 'Oh give me the comfort of thy help again', and suggested:

Restore unto me the joy of thy salvation:
And uphold me with a free spirit.

We need a word like 'restore' because there are times in life when this exuberance is clouded, and this joy seems to be witheld. But in personal relationships there is no human joy so deep as that which comes from knowing that we are forgiven and loved and accepted, and the same is true when our relationship with God is in some way renewed. No wonder the psalmist uses the vivid metaphor of broken bones dancing!

We cannot know the reality of forgiveness until we know the reality of sin. But it is no part of our Christian calling to wallow in sin. Rather does its acknowledgement lead to pardon, cleansing and joy. Through realism about nature we come to the wonder of grace.

LENT

INSIGHTS FROM THE PSALMS

4 Confidence — Psalm 121

We come today to one of the best-known and most-loved of the
Psalms. But it is also one of the most misunderstood. It is misunderstood not because the thought is difficult; it is fairly simple.
Nor is the translation of the Prayer Book obscure; it is fairly plain.
It is misunderstood because the punctuation is wrong. It has been
put right in modern versions. But in the Authorised Version, the
Book of Common Prayer and the Scottish Metrical Psalter, there
is a question-mark missing from the end of the first verse. The
psalmist did not say 'I will lift up mine eyes to the hills because I
shall find help there.' He asked a question:

> I will lift up mine eyes to the hills;
> But where shall I find help?

And the rest of the Psalm is an answer to the question posed in the
first verse.

That bit of punctuation is important. You see, you don't find
God in nature unless you have already found him somewhere
else. The hills themselves are neutral. Sometimes they seem to
suggest the divine, sometimes the demonic. If you visit the
churchyard at Wasdale Head, which is situated in one of the most
awesome parts of the Lake District, you will find on the grave of
a young climber the opening words of this Psalm 'I will lift up
mine eyes to the hills.' They could have been ironic; for it was the
hills that killed that young man. But God can speak to you on the
hills only if you know the kind of God who is speaking. The hills,
I repeat are, in themselves neutral. Indeed, some commentators
think that the psalmist viewed the hills as the sanctuaries of other
cults, and knew that deliverance must come from beyond them.
And the inscription on the tombstone is hopeful only in the light
of the rest of the Psalm.

Now follow a series of little similes about the divine protection
— which the psalmist has learned not from his contemplation of

the hills, but from the experience of his people in their history. He is the one who does not sleep; the consistency of his love and care are beyond the kindness of the best of fellow-pilgrims. He is the defence at our right hand — at once closer and more alert than any human companion. He watches for the pitfalls along the way; he is like a shade to protect from sunstroke, or what were considered in the ancient world to be the baleful effects of the moon. He watches our coming in and our going out — a rich symbol, echoed many times in the Bible.

In these verses, we see what the divine protection is *like*. But what does it *do*? And in what sense is this a Psalm of confidence?

This was a favourite Psalm of two great nineteenth century missionaries. When David Livingstone left his home at Blantyre, the family rose at five o'clock, his mother made coffee, and then they read this Psalm. There was a sense in which Livingstone was protected, for his explorations lasted some thirty years. But they finally wore him out, and he was certainly subject to the perils of his journeys. James Hannington, first Bishop of what was then called Equatorial Africa, was murdered at the age of 37. His diaries are full of allusions to the Psalms; and this one (which he called the Traveller's Psalm) he read every day of the journey that led to his death.

Were such men buoyed up by false hopes? Certainly the Psalm did not prove literally true for either of them. Or could it be that it is speaking of a security for the inner being, the real self, the soul? If so, then it almost anticipates that great passage in St Paul's letter to the Romans where he tells us that neither life nor death, nor angels, nor principalities nor powers, nor things present nor things to come, nor height nor depth nor any other creature shall be able to separate us from the love of God, which is in Christ Jesus our Lord. The psalmist knows nothing of Jesus Christ our Lord; nor does he have any firm notion of a life beyond this one. But one of the most impressive features of the Old Testament is the conviction that God is in control. He is faithful, and his will must be done. This conviction has sustained the people of Israel in their long and troubled history. You could say that it often puts us to shame.

But this is where our confidence rests. It is not a confidence in protection against all life's accidents. We are still prone to the slings and arrows of outrageous fortune. As Kenneth Slack has written, 'If God's guardianship was literal deliverance, why did he not put his chosen people on some remote island in the South Seas? . . . Instead, he led them to a promised land which was just a bridge, the narrow fertile strip between sea and desert, the ends of which rested in the great empires of the era. So across the land — the *promised* land — empires would tramp, and the people in it would be in the cockpit of history. What a strange guardian of Israel!

Yet Israel's greatest Son, Jesus our Lord, recited this Psalm as did the other pilgrims on the way to Jerusalem. Through what happened there he confirms that which the psalmist has hinted at; that you and I are precious to God, and that no matter what happens to us, our real selves are safe in him.

LENT

INSIGHTS FROM THE PSALMS

5 Adoration — Psalm 148

When I was a small boy, I was always fascinated by verse 10 of the Psalm that we are going to look at today — Psalm 148: 'Beasts and all cattle: worms and feathered fowls!' I always wondered how a worm managed to praise God. Did it get up on its end, and then curl over in adoration? I didn't ask the same question about beasts and all cattle, or about the feathered fowls. It was the worm that I worried about.

In our worship, we often express the sentiments of this Psalm. It belongs to a whole group of nature-songs in which the whole creation is invited to join in the praise of God. This particular Psalm bears a resemblance to the Benedicite from the Apocrypha. The first six verses call on the heavenly beings to praise God; not only the angels, but sun, moon and stars can offer him praise after their own mode. Verses 7 to 10 address the summons to the things of earth — mountains and hills as well as sea-monsters and creeping things. Only when we get to verse 11 do people come into the picture — kings and judges, young men and maidens, old men and children. The final verses give the reason for this outburst of adoration — his name only is excellent. In the Old Testament, the name always denotes character. As we saw in our study of Psalm 121, the psalmist finds God in nature because he has been found already in the history and experience of his people Israel. To that people he gives victory, or they find their victory in him; the 'horn' (verse 14) is a symbol of that victory.

We often sing Psalms and hymns of this sort. Are they simply poetry, or do we mean something more when we praise him in this way? Certainly this Psalm is poetry; and if we approach it with a literal mind, we may find it difficult to understand how hail manages to praise God, let alone the worm! But I think this nature-psalm points us to truths beyond itself, and to these we now turn.

First then, the Psalm helps us to see our setting in creation. We noted that it is not until verse 11 that the psalmist mentions men and women. That puts us in our place — the place where we ought to be. Do you remember the great chapters with which the book of Job end? Job never gets an answer to his questions; but instead he is shown a panorama of nature, and in the course of it minute descriptions of the habits of the ostrich and the mountain-goat. We are apt to be preoccupied with ourselves as though we were the only part of creation that mattered. But sometimes children light on truths to which their elders are blind. Albert Schweitzer, known in this century alternately as theologian and doctor recalls that when he was a child he found it incomprehensible that one should pray only for human beings, and as soon as his mother had gone, he used to add silently a prayer for the creatures. In recent years, many voices have been recalling us to the importance of the environment in which we dwell; and others warn us that if we lose contact with nature we shall lose our moorings, for we shall be cut off from that to which we belong. Nature is to be neither ignored nor patronised, for in it we see the glory of God. Everyone knows the lines from Elizabeth Barrett Browning:

Earth's crammed with heaven
And every common bush afire with God.

But not so many remember what follows:

But only he who sees takes off his shoes;
The rest sit round it and pluck blackberries.

Secondly, the psalmist speaks of the diversity of creation. In Gloucester Cathedral, a plaque has recently been put up in memory of the poet of the Forest of Dean, F. W. Harvey. On this theme he wrote:

When God had finished the stars and whirl of coloured suns,
He turned his mind from big things, to fashion little ones,
Beautiful tiny things (like daisies) he made, and then
He made the comical ones, in case the minds of men
       Should stiffen, and become
       Dull, humourless and glum,
       And so forgetful of their Maker be
       As to take themselves — quite seriously.
Caterpillars and cats are likely and excellent puns.
All God's jokes are good, even the practical ones.
And as for the duck, I think God must have smiled
Seeing those bright eyes blink on the day he fashioned it
       And He's probably laughing still
       At the sound that came out of its bill.

Diversity in the natural order leads to diversity in the human species. There are all sorts of ways of praising God, and the psalmist hints that the way of the judge may not be the way of the young men and maidens, that what is appropriate for old men may not be appropriate for children. All sorts of people are needed — in the Church as well as in the world. Too often we make stereotypes, and identify what is Christian with the *mores* of that bit of society with which we are identified — whether it be middle-class attitudes or revolutionary aspirations. By so doing, we deny the diversity intended for the human race and the diversity of praise which they can offer to the Creator.

The psalmist has said all that he can say. Yet he hints at something more — something that we find explicit in other parts of the Old Testament as well as the New. There is a reminder of our setting in creation; an exploration of the diversity of creation but maybe also a longing for the perfecting of creation. So Isaiah speaks of the harmony in the created order which Messiah will bring; St Paul of the redemption in store for the whole creation; and John of Patmos of the new heaven and the new earth. What these things can mean is largely hidden from us. What they show us is that our slavation is not *from* the created order, but *with* it. And any form of Christianity which is limited to what is called the 'spiritual' is a poor shadow of the gospel of him whose love is over all his works.

'Man's chief end is to glorify God and enjoy him for ever'. So runs the Westminster Confession. We glorify him not only by our formal songs in church and occasional uplifting thoughts outside. We glorify him by being ourselves — the selves that he made, redeemed and will perfect. We do this in the company not only of the hosts of heaven, but of the whole created order which reflects his glory and will share his victory.

MAUNDY THURSDAY

There is, I think, one fringe sect which celebrates Holy Communion only once a year — on this day. We who celebrate it frequently find this occasion unique in the year. The words 'In the same night as he was betrayed' have a directness that we probably do not regularly experience. We seem to be in the Upper Room itself.

It is therefore surprising that the Gospel from which we have just read contains no reference to the institution of the Eucharist. Many reasons have been advanced for St John's omission of this event. One is that he assumes that his readers will know about it already since it is the basis of their normal worship. Another is that he is anxious to prevent this knowledge from coming to pagan eyes. Most convicing is the suggestion that he prefers to talk about such things in a different way. For although he does not actually describe the sacrament, he seems to have more to say about it than the other three evangelists put together.

What he does do is to spell out another activity which took place in the Upper Room. He alone gives us the incomparable story of the feet-washing. And in his chronology, this takes place not on the Passover, but on its eve; and the occasion is a semi-religious, semi-social event (as we should describe it) for which groups of friends might meet on this occasion.

So, for the lessons tonight, we have St Paul's account of the Eucharist set beside St John's account of the feet-washing. And the two belong together. They tell us that communion with Christ means service to one another. They tell us that those who want to serve Christ in their fellows must be prepared to receive him themselves.

It is tragic when these two aspect of Christian discipleship are, as it were, set against each other. It is tragic when the evangelical and social gospels are seen as alternatives. You can see how this happens. When the Church becomes an end in itself, when its members seem preoccupied with their own affairs, then we need to hear the prophetic voices which tell us that Christ is to be found among the needy and the anonymous. But when Christianity seems to become synonymous with social welfare, then we need to hear the priestly voices which tell us that we do not live by bread alone, that the Church's discipline of prayer and sacrament is in fact the unique thing that she has to offer to the world.

Older people here have seen the pendulum swing both ways. When the Welfare State was set up, it seemed that the Church's role in welfare was at an end. There was no further need for the loaves or coals provided by the will of some eighteenth century benefactor, or for their more modern counterpart, and it is only the drop-outs who call at the Vicarage for this sort of help. But after a decade in which the Church's main interests had been in her own structures, her worship and her unity, there arose prophets who pointed to famine and underdevelopment abroad, and to great yawning gaps in the Welfare State at home.

It is better that the pendulum should go on swinging than that it should stand still. But the social and devotional aspects of the Gospel belong together. They are two sides of a coin. When we receive the Lord in the Sacrament, we allow him to live in us; and then it is that we see the world with his eyes, and walk in it with his feet. But to work in the world, even for him, is to discover pretty quickly how frail is our love, how fickle our desire to minister to other people. And then we see once again our need of that strength and grace that can come only from him. In short, Christ forces us out into the world; but the world forces us back to him.

Tonight we are reminded that the hands which took bread are the hands that took a towel. He who does these things for us tells us that these are the things which we must do for one another. Breaking bread in the sanctuary means sharing bread in the world. To be one with Christ at his table is to be one with him in his sacrificial love. This is why our modern liturgies, like the ancient ones, end rather abruptly. When we have received communion, we must go and work out its implications. This is the proper response to 'Go in peace and serve the Lord' — not another hymn, or more prayers, but actually going out to be his Body in the world for which he died.

What we are doing here we often call 'a service.' It is significant that we use the same word for what we shall do when it is over.

PASSIONTIDE

1 The Cross Foreshadowed

Readings: Isaiah 52. 13–53. 12; 63. 7–9; Hosea 11. 1–9; Luke 24. 25–27

St Luke is not alone in insisting that what happened to Jesus was in accordance with the Scriptures — the Old Testament. St John concludes his proclamation of the resurrection with the words 'Until then they had not understood the Scriptures which showed that he must rise from the dead.' When St Paul recorded 'the facts which had been imparted to me' the first was 'that Christ died for our sins, according to the Scriptures.'

It is likely that the Scriptures to which these writers refer included the passages which we have just read. Certainly, some of them sound uncannily prophetic of what happened to Jesus. It was necessary for the New Testament writers to refer back in the way that they did — in order to demonstrate that Jesus was the expected Messiah. But doesn't the case depend upon a very careful selection of passages? Can you really show from the Old Testament that the sufferings of Christ were in some way foretold — or even that they are of a piece with what is written there?

I think it would be foolish to claim that the Old Testament is monochrome in its witness, or that the picture of God that we find there is unchanging and consistent. In the second passage that we read, the Lord is identified with his people in their sufferings — 'in all their affliction, he was afflicted.' But it follows a passage in which the Deliverer is described as One who tramples nations in his fury, and sheds blood in his anger. In any case, we realise that in the Old Testament, we have a very varied collection of material. It includes poetry, history, myth and saga. It belongs to a wide range of dates and circumstances. It is only the printing of Bibles that makes it seem uniform.

Yet when we have said all this, there is one strain which runs through many books of the Old Testament. It is a strain which suggests that hope and restoration come through suffering and loss. It has certainly been grasped by the people to whom these books originally belonged. It is this belief that has sustained and inspired Jews in their turbulent history. And one of the classics of twentieth century theology is Wheeler Robinson's *The Cross in the Old Testament*. Of course, this is only one theme of the Old Testament; but it is a theme, a persistent theme. And for Christians who believe that the fullness of relevation came through Jesus, it is an enduring theme.

But why do we need to establish it? What does it matter? It matters for this reason: whatever you believe about Christianity depends on what you believe about God. The Christian faith is concerned in the first place not with whether you believe in God, but with what *kind* of God you believe in? If you think that the majority of mankind is destined for Hell, or that the only valid church is one governed by bishops, then you must ask the question 'What kind of God wills such things?'. Perhaps the most bitter words ever addressed by one Christian to another were those of John Wesley when he said 'Your God is my devil.'

When we see Jesus lifted on his cross, we see God; — not just part of God, not just God, as it were, in a good mood. We see the meaning of things disclosed in these events. The padre and poet of the first World War, Geoffrey Studdert-Kennedy put it this way:

> God, the God I love and worship, reigns in sorrow on the Tree,
> Broken, bleeding, but unconquered, very God of God to me.
>
> . . .
>
> High and lifted up I see Him on the eternal Calvary,
> And two pierced hands are stretching east and west o'er land and sea,
> On my knees I fall and worship that great Cross that shines above,
> For the very God of Heaven is not Power, but Power of Love.

Now I know that this word 'love' has been so trivialised, cheapened and sentimentalised, that you almost hesitate to use it. But here it is — something that we partly understand, partly don't. It corresponds with what lies deepest in us all, yet in its fullness is beyond our understanding and experience. This is at the heart of all things, this is the essence of what is revealed in Christ. Much else there is to be said about him; but always we come back to this.

In Mrs Gaskell's *Ruth*, there is a character called Mr Bradshaw. Although he was a devout and staunch chapel-goer, he seemed to have missed the first thing that any Christian ought to know — that we are all sinners in need of God's forgiveness. It was only through suffering that he was softened; and not until the very end of the book are love and compassion revealed in the man.

This is certainly not an analogy of God as he is; but it is an analogy of God as men have sometimes seen him — even in the Old

Testament itself. Love is the final description of what he is — but this becomes clear to us through the Cross as in no other way. Of course he is a God of righteousness, a God of judgement. Often we see only clouds and darkness round about him. Often with Cowper, the smiling face is hidden behind a frowning Providence. But he is a God who is always identified with his people, always seeking to communicate with them. Neither can be done without suffering; and therefore the love which is vulnerable, the love which knows no limits is that which claims our worship and our obedience. This is our God. And therefore before ever there was a cross on a hill called Calvary, there was a cross in the heart of God.

PASSIONTIDE

2 The Cross Described

Readings: St Mark 15. 21–39; St Luke 23. 26–48; St John 19. 17–37

In reading these three accounts of the crucifixion, we have followed the good example of the Prayer Book which in turn rested upon the traditional practice of the Western Church — that of reading all four Passion narratives during the services of Holy Week.

This still has considerable value for us. For it shows us first, the substantial agreement between the four evangelists and, secondly, the different insights and distinctive emphases that each one draws out. Let's look first at the mesure of agreement. Each Gospel begins with the story of the Upper Room, goes on to the **Kedron Valley or Gethsemane, describes the trials before the** Sanhedrin and under Pontius Pilate, records with varying detail the scene on the *Via Dolorosa*, and sets forth the crucifixion. Because the same basic outline is found in all four Gospels, people have thought it proper to conflate them, and to make one story. This is the way in which Passion plays old and new are often constructed; on these lines, the traditional Three Hours Devotion is planned.

But in recent years there have been New Testament scholars who have warned us against doing it this way. Many great composers have written choral settings for the Requiem Mass, and they used a basic text for their work. But can you imagine a concert consisting of Mozart's *Dies Irae,* Fauré's *Sanctus* and Verdi's *Agnus Dei*? Not many people attend the Requiems in order to learn more about the rite that inspired them, yet it is true that the composer is using both text and music to convey something that he wants us to hear. So it is with the evangelists who record the story of the crucifixion.

So we turn to the differences. The most striking is in the words ascribed to Jesus. In Mark (closely followed by Matthew) — there is only one terrible saying from the Cross 'My God, my God, why hast thou forsaken me?' The rejected Messiah is the theme of this account. Luke gives us three 'words'; 'Father forgive'; 'Today thou shalt be with me in Paradise'; 'Father, into thy hands I commit my spirit' — words of mercy, acceptance, trust. St John has another three 'Woman, behold thy son. . .'; 'I thirst' (in a Gospel which has spoken much of water); 'It is finished' — words of glory and of victory.

Nor are these the only differences. John has no account of the Last Supper, but a description of Jesus washing the feet of his disciples. Luke tells of women wailing as Jesus carries his Cross to Calvary, and Matthew ends his story with an earthquake so powerful that even the graves were torn open.

Why do I emphasise both the similarities and the differences in the accounts? First, because I want you to be assured of the historicity of what you read. It did happen — in the way described. Many people exaggerate the differences, and suppose that because the accounts vary, we cannot be sure about any one of them. Now the things that the evangelists have in common are more than those on which they differ. But as we think of the last hours of Jesus' life and try to meditate on them, how do we know which account is most accurate — Mark, Luke or John? We cannot know this. Maybe Jesus spoke all seven words — maybe he spoke more, and these are all that remain. Maybe the words that we read are what a particular writer thought the scene was saying to him.

I think we can live with some uncertainty about that. But more positively, I am sure that we can rejoice in the diversity that we have. The different ways in which the Cross is described is not a disadvantage, but an advantage. We need to hear the different things that they are saying. We need to appreciate the dereliction that we find in Mark. We need to know that Jesus had indeed plumbed the depths of physical and mental suffering — in order to know now that he can save to the uttermost. We need also the words which Luke gives in his account of the crucifixion — words of forgiveness, acceptance, trust — for on such things each one of us depends. And we need John's emphasis on the glory and victory of it all; for through him we are shown that this is not just a tragic story that is all put right on Easter Day, but that God is in it all, and the Cross is the instrument of his victory. Each account speaks not only to the mind, but to the soul. The separate accounts of the crucifixion bring home to us the different sides of the truth. Sometimes it will be one evangelist who will speak to our condition, sometimes another; and together they speak of the adequacy for each one of us what God has done in Christ.

And so here in the Gospels themselves, we find the starting point of the many-sidedness of Christ's work upon the Cross. On this men and women have meditated through the Christian centuries, and have used music and art and words to reveal what they have seen. This great company we now join as we hear the Cross described and take our place at its foot.

PASSIONTIDE

3 The Cross Interpreted

Readings: Col. 2. 9–15; Heb. 9. 11–15, 23–28; 10. 19–25; 2 Cor. 5. 18–21

We were looking last time at the Cross described — described by three evangelists. You must have noticed that in all four Gospels, a considerable proportion of the story is taken up with the death of Christ. The writers were concerned not just to investigate details, but to declare the significance of what happened on Calvary.

They had a hard case to prove. It was hard to persuade their fellow-Jews that Jesus was the Messiah. For this Messiah died in ignominy and shame. When people expected the Messiah's life would culminate in earthly victory, it was difficult to convince them that a man who had died on a Cross ordered by a Roman governor could in fact be the Messiah. Those problems are not ours — precisely; yet it is still difficult to understand why the Cross is the symbol and means of God's purpose.

Yet the first Christians believed that in some way this crucifixion was part of God's plan, and that Christ had died for their sins. We have just read extracts from other writers in the New Testament who tried to interpret the Cross. As we might expect, the ways in which they sought to explain it arose from their own culture and religion. They thought of Adam as the source of human sin; so Christ became the 'second Adam' annulling the transgressions of the past. Religion in Jerusalem centred around temple, priesthood and sacrifice; so Christ became both the new High Priest and the perfect victim for sacrifice. They thought of a world in bondage to Satan and constantly distorted by devils; so Christ is seen as the victor over all the powers of evil.

Thus we notice two things: that right from the beginning, there was a pluriform understanding of what Christ had achieved on the Cross, and that there was a highly symbolic method of describing it. So it has been through the Christian centuries as men and women have wrestled with the meaning of what we call the Atonement. On this theme, there have been many books, many sermons and many lectures. And others have approached it not through words, but through symbols — in art and sculpture, in music and drama, in poetry and myth. The truth for which they have striven is always in some sense elusive, for it is a truth that can never be tied down to explanations.

The Church, as a whole, has never been committed to any of the analogies — ancient or modern — by which her sons have interpreted the Cross. There has been the analogy of the slave-market, and the idea of ransom; there has been the analogy of the law-court, and the idea of acquittal for the guilty; there has been the analogy of the temple, and the idea of the perfect victim. Admittedly, some Christians have come near to saying 'You must understand and believe it *this* way' and some still come near to saying it. But the wiser word was spoken by C.S. Lewis, 'You can say that Christ died for our sins. You may say that the Father has forgiven us because Christ has done for us what we ought to have done. You may say that we are washed in the blood of the Lamb. You may say that Christ has defeated death. They are all true. If any one of them does not appeal to you leave it alone and get on with the formula that does. And, whatever you do, do not start quarrelling with other people because they use a different formula from yours.' To this we can add some further wise words by the nineteenth century theologian, F. J. A. Hort, who speaks of Atonement as, 'a region into which we have only glimpses, and all figures taken from things below are of necessity partial and imperfect. It is far better to accept a theology that leaves us puzzled than to buy clarity at the cost of inadequacy.'

To put it crudely, we do not know what difference the Cross made to God. In our first address, we thought of the Cross in his heart before there was one on Calvary, and we saw that his nature and his name is love, that in the words of the old prayer, 'his property is always to have mercy.' The majority of Christian theologians have always wanted to insist that something objective happened on the Cross, and that it was more than a demonstration of God's forgiveness. But we have noted the limitations of all ways of describing this. We cannot explain the difference it makes to God.

But we do know the difference that it makes to us. I can start quite simply with my own self and you can start with yours. I know my need of forgiveness and acceptance. I know that this Cross draws me from my self-centredness and waywardness. But more than this, you and I look out on a world of sorrow and pain on problems that seem insoluble; on a society that seems fettered by ropes of iron. Only a divine initiative can break this. That initiative we see on the Cross.

We see Christ hanging there because of the actions of men —
not just individuals, but of societies and their past. He hangs there
because of fear, because of indifference, because of pride, because
of jealousy. And all these things that we find in people and in
communities are there partly because of what others have done to
them. That is why you can never find a culprit on Good Friday.
As Sydney Carter sang 'You can blame it on to Pilate, you can
blame it on the Jews', but it always goes deeper, always goes
beyond those on whom you apportion blame. All the world's evil
and sorrow, its stunted growth and its perennial frustrations are
focussed there. This is what it all came to, this is what it comes to
again and again.

And yet we see One who triumphed over it. We see a love that
could not be extinguished or warped, a life that could not be
destroyed. This love is indestructible. And in all its apparent
weakness and vulnerability, it is shown as stronger than the
imperial powers or implacable hatreds of this world.

This is one way of looking at the Cross. And without the Cross
I do not know how we could see such things.

PASSIONTIDE

4 The Cross Proclaimed

Readings: Act 2. 22–36; 8. 26–36; 1 Cor. 1. 21–24; Rev. 5. 1–10

Nobody is now startled by a cross. It has become an ineradicable
part of the world's culture. No one can count the times in which it
has been portrayed in oils, in stone, in wood or glass. No one can
count the number of times it comes in the language of devotion —
in hymns and prayers and anthems. It goes on being manufac-
tured, multiplied in churches, embroidered on linen, worn
around the neck. It is one of the earliest things associated with
baptism; until recent times, it commonly marked the resting-
places of the dead.

Doubtless its familiarity has dulled its significance. And there
have been ways of proclaiming the Cross that have obscured its

meaning. There have been wars fought in its cause, crusades undertaken in its honour, which have made it seem one power among many. Yet as we have seen, the power of the Cross lies in its defencelessness — in the love that submitted to death, but could not be destroyed by it.

What difference does this kind of belief make to our attitude and actions? It means, first, that we are all debtors, all sinners, all in need. In many of our human complaints, it is as we identify and acknowledge our need that we are open to help and healing. This is certainly true of our relationship with God. Charles Wesley expresses this in almost every hymn he wrote; and one of the greatest is that based on the story of wrestling Jacob:

> What though my shrinking flesh complain
> And murmur to contend so long,
> I rise, superior to my pain,
> When I am weak, then I am strong
> And when my all of strength shall fail,
> I shall with the God-man prevail.

To accept God's forgiveness and to realise his acceptance has important by-products. We don't have to struggle to be something or to prove something. We can more readily accept limitations, admit failures, be human. That does not mean mere passivity. It means rather than we are open to God, open to all that he can do in us and with us — knowing that we find ourselves only as we are found by him, knowing that we realise our potential only as we are united with him.

Then it is that we are able to carry our cross — not in some spirit of grim duty or enforced martyrdom, but because we know that only through love and forgiveness is anything worthwhile achieved. This is the true proclamation of the Cross, and, as we have seen, there have been many false ones. Because we are mixed-up people, there is likely to be a mixture of the true and the false in our own witness. One of the fathers of Anglicanism, Richard Hooker, once said very gently, 'The best things we do have somewhat in them to be pardoned.'

Yet the Cross has been proclaimed by fallible men and women. Students of modern church history often try to examine the question of how far nineteenth century missionary activity was a reflection of western imperialism. Many come to the conclusion that it was — at least, in part. Yet the stories of the missionaries themselves often reveal unquestioned devotion and genuine heroism. Their lives as well as their words were a proclamation of the Cross.

But the Cross has been proclaimed in other ways. Not least of them is to be found in the undramatic and largely unchronicled lives of Christian men and women. I do not refer to the pretentious or the smug, to paraded devotion or ostentatious charity. I speak instead of those who have really taken Christ at his word; to those who really have believed that the way of the Cross was the way of hope for their world, and lived by that conviction. We may think of people who have made real but unobtrusive sacrifices of their time, their energies, or their money; of people who have been willing to be misrepresented or misunderstood; of people who have born pain and frustration, yet have not allowed these things to poison their outlook or their relationships. And as I speak of such people, you will yourselves be supplying their names, for some such you have known. They have found the Cross to be the way that led to joy and peace — though they might never have used such language about themselves. The peace to which they have come and the joy which has been found in them are not as the world understands these things. As Douglas Webster has written: 'There was no applauding audience at Calvary. Only God and Mary and the angels knew what was happening. So it will often be with the Christian disciple, if it is the Cross he chooses and not the centre of the stage.'

So we take our place among those who have proclaimed the Cross — in word and deed. 'Jesus hath many lovers of his Kingdom but few bearers of his Cross,' wrote Thomas à Kempis back in the fifteenth century. But the Kingdom is made visible, its boundaries enlarged, its boundaries enlarged, its power experienced only as poeple like ourselves take up and proclaim the Cross. We do this not lamenting our minority status, not chalking up our successes, but simply by our obedience to the symbol and means of the world's salvation.

EASTER

1 Corinthians 5.7 Christ our Passover has been sacrificed for us; so let us celebrate the feast.

Jesus was crucified during the Passover festival. As Christians began to realise the significance of what had happened, so they transferred to him, crucified and risen, all the associations of Passover. The deliverance from Egypt, the crossing of the Red Sea, and the entry into the Promised Land — all this had happened again, and in an even more wonderful way than at the first Passover.

So it is that we, who meet in the British Isles on a Spring morning, find ourselves — rather curiously — reciting place-names from the Middle East. The names have become familiar enough to this generation, since the Middle East has so often featured in the news. But now we use those names in our worship. Not only do we read passages from the Old Testament that deal with Passover, but we sing specifically Christian hymns that echo its themes. Thus:

> Loosed from Pharoah's bitter yoke
> Jacob's sons and daughters;
> Led them with unmoistened feet
> Through the Red Sea waters.

or

> Ye choirs of new Jerusalem,
> Your sweetest notes employ
> The Paschal victory to hymn
> In strains of holy joy.

But isn't all this a rather roundabout way of celebrating Easter? Why, as someone asked the other day do we have to be constantly harping on these old Jews? Can't we understand and rejoice in the

Resurrection without all this Old Testament background? Well, maybe we can. But I believe that these symbolic names can give depth to our thoughts today, and that is why I invite you to look at three of them with me.

First then, we look at Egypt, the place of bondage. Egypt gets a raw deal in the Bible. There is no recognition of its rich and rare civilisation. There is not much gratitude for the fact that the people of Israel were sustained by its corn. It is seen as a source of oppression, a centre of bondage — which indeed it became. It is freedom from the yoke of slavery that people celebrated at Passover.

Perhaps the biblical writers exaggerated the evils of Eygpt. Certainly there are forms of Christian proclamation that exaggerate the evils of this world. We think it cannot be so bad when we worship in beautiful buildings or walk through pleasant gardens, or have people we love around us. Yet it remains true that with all its beauty, its wonder and its goodness, this world is still under the sway of what theologians call sin and everyone calls death. Something happens to show us that the civilisation we value is but a thin veneer over primitive forces. Something **happens to bring home to us the almost insupportable transience of** all things — including ourselves and what we love. And this is bondage — for us all. No doubt some of those individual Jewish slaves carried particular and bitter burdens; and so do some of you. This is why we may speak of Egypt, speak of our need of deliverance. It is a need of all of us; if you do not feel it today, you very well may feel it tomorrow.

So we come to the Red Sea, the place of deliverance. The details of the first Passover are strange and confusing — the blood on the door-posts, the lamb eaten in haste, the swirling waters of the Red Sea. No less mysterious is the process by which we have been set free — the anguish of Gethsemane, the agony of crucifixion, the unimaginable experience which the Church sought to incapsulate in the phrase 'He descended into hell.' There is no formula by which we can describe to our own satisfaction (or to anyone else's) the full meaning of our redemption in Christ. We have only partial explanations and opaque symbols. That Christ died for our sins has been the confession of Christians over many centuries; that we receive newness of life through him is their experience today.

So we look to Canaan, the place of promise. Men and women have always looked to some Utopia — not least men and women from that race which we have been considering. But Canaan, the Promised Land, does not provide us with tidy answers or neat solutions to the apparently insoluble problems of the Creation. It speaks instead of a realm in which sin and death are no more because the love of God is all in all. We are already citizens of that realm. We are already in possession of eternal life, because Christ has set us free from every form of bondage — those which we know, and those of which we are hardly aware. Christ our Passover has been sacrificed for us; so let us celebrate the feast.

It all sounds good. It may even sound convincing — on a Spring morning and at an Anglican Easter. But most of us know that life won't always feel like this, because it doesn't always feel like this. So let me mention one more symbolic place, the wilderness. Between the Red Sea and the Promised Land, there was the journey through the wilderness. Sometimes, in the biblical narrative, the people forgot the wonder of the Red Sea and longed for the security of Egypt. And often we look back — wondering if our faith is valid, wondering whether people who don't share it are better off than ourselves. If thoughts like that cloud this Easter Day for you, then remember the *hopeless* bondage is past, you *have* crossed that sea, all that God has for you is ahead. For Christ has risen; the new Passover is ours; so let us celebrate the feast.

ASCENSION

Acts 1. 9 A cloud received him from their sight.

The New Testament writers are reticent about the event of the Ascension. They have much to say about its significance, but not much more than this about what happened. At the end of St Luke's Gospel. Jesus is simply 'parted from' his disciples. Here in the Acts of the Apostles 'a cloud received him from their sight.' It

54

is true that revelations about where he was going and how he would come again accompanied the biblical account. But it was left to later writers and artists to elaborate on this in a way that has made it a 'problem' for some. Thus the bench-end of a Cornish church shows feet disappearing at the top, and footmarks at the bottom. But Luke speaks of what is an every-day occurence on mountains — the cloud suddenly descending, the visibility almost totally gone. Yet he is using a word that carried deep meanings for his readers, and to this we must turn.

The cloud is the means of separation. The disciples realised that they would not see Jesus in the way they had seen him. He had been taken away. He had gone from them. I once heard a sermon on Ascension Day with which I violently disagreed at the time. But you don't have to agree with a sermon in order to benefit from it, and that one certainly made me think again. The preacher said that Ascension Day presented us with the 'real absence' of Jesus. And in one sense this is so. The Jesus who lived two thousand years ago has gone, has not been seen again. So the cloud speaks to us of separation — of the reality of parting, of endings, of death itself, and it does not minimise the sorrow of these things. Moreover, the psalmist speaks of 'clouds and dark-ness' round about God Himself, and sometimes we are conscious only of the distance between ourselves and him.

Yet in the thought of the Bible, the cloud is most commonly the symbol of God's presence. There was the cloud by day that accompanied the ancient people as they went through the wilder-ness, and there was the cloud which hung over Moses in his encounter with the Lord. A cloud was seen on the Mount of Transfiguration, and it is on clouds of heaven that Jesus is said to return. So the cloud which is in human terms the means of separation is in divine terms the sign of God's presence.

This paradox is all of a place with what is recorded about the events of Christ. There was no room in the inn. God was shut out. Yet the bare manger which seems to deny the splendour of God is in fact the expression of it. The Cross represents the ultimate in ignominy for any human being; yet here where Christ seems to be defeated, it is here that he reigns. It is in those very places where God seems most obviously absent that he is in fact most really present.

When we understand this, then we are more able to cope with our own problems. The cloud so often threatens to destroy our equanimity or happiness. It may be the cloud of doubt or perplexity, or the cloud of sorrow and loneliness. It is at such times we say 'Why did God do this to me?' or, perhaps more often we wonder whether there is a God at all. The symbolism of the cloud does not suggest that what we are going through is unreal or trivial. But it does speak of God supremely revealed in the Man of Sorrows. It does speak of grace in time of weakness, of resurrection beyond death.

Let me end with two illustrations of how this has been seen. In the fourteenth century, an unknown English mystic wrote a treatise called *The Cloud of Unknowing*. It is not easy to read, and some of it is not easy to accept. The writer sees the cloud that stands in the way of contemplation as something that cannot be pierced by reason, but only by love. And he writes, 'This darkness and this cloud, howsoever thou dost, is betwixt thee and thy God, and hindereth thee, so thou mayest neither see him clearly by light of understanding in thy reason, nor feel him in sweetness of love in thine affection. And therefore shape thee to bide in this darkness as long as thou mayest, ever more crying after him whom thou lovest. For if ever thou shalt see him or feel him, as it may be here, it must always be in this cloud and this darkness.'

A hard saying! But in 1865, during the Cotton Famine in Lancashire, a mill-owner called the workers together and told them that the mill must close. A bitter silence fell on those people. Hope and confidence seemed lost. Yet hope was somehow rekindled and the silence broken, by the voice of a girl who sang:

> Ye fearful saints, fresh courage take,
> The clouds ye so much dread
> Are big with mercy, and shall break
> In blessings on your head.

PENTECOST

Just outside Oxford there is a property of the Open University. For many years before, the house and grounds belonged to Ripon Hall, a theological college of our Church. The students were privileged to live in an incomparable setting; there were lawns and woods, and in the middle of them a small stretch of water dignified with the name 'lake'. Around it, in the Summer term, blossomed rhododendrons of many shades of red and pink. We always hoped that a particularly brilliant red variety would come out in time for Whit Sunday, and so go to decorate a church in the city.

But sometimes the rhododendrons did not oblige. It depended on the weather and the time of Easter. Often we had to make do with other shades of red. Those who have decorated the church today will sympathise. It is not always easy to get the traditional flowers of Whitsun — the colours of flame, which symbolise the fire of the Spirit.

Yet the softer reds have their own lesson to teach. The activity of God the Holy Spirit cannot be symbolised by one colour, because that activity is manifold. Whatever lectionary we use, we always read on this day the passage from the Acts of the Apostles that describes events on the day of Pentecost. There is an atmosphere of disturbance and exhilaration. Turn to the Gospel — again always from St John on this day, and the Holy Spirit is given to those who are faithful and obedient to Christ, and there is less sense of drama. In the letter to the Romans, it is the Spirit who assures us that we are children of God and enables us to live as such, and in the letter to the Galatians he is the source of such virtues as gentleness or goodness. And in at least two places, St Paul makes it clear that the gifts of the Spirit are varied — surely because the activity of the Spirit is varied.

I want to underline this point, because so often in Christian history the Holy Spirit has been either ignored or misunderstood. Thank God we do not live in days when he is ignored; he is not now generally understood as some vague influence or optional extra to Christianity. The real strength of a church can be seen not in the Christmas or Easter communicants, but in those of Whit Sunday. There has been a revival of interest in the Holy Spirit — through the charismatic movement. His presence and power has been experienced in groups that meet for fellowship and healing. He is most certainly there, but he is elsewhere also. He is in all places of reconciliation and healing. The Holy Spirit is misunderstood when people try to tie him down, and make him their own peculiar property. The Holy Spirit is not the property of sects or parties, nor yet of churches and religions.

For the Holy Spirit is so much greater: he is God in action, God in the present. We live in the age of the Spirit. This is one reason why the remaining Sundays of the Christian Year are now called 'Sundays after Pentecost'. It is through the Holy Spirit that God now seeks to communicate with men and women. For that reason alone, his activity must be manifold. At one moment, he needs to shake us out of our complacency; at another he seeks to settle and stablise us. Sometimes he is revealing to us new truths at which neither we nor our fathers guessed; but somes it is old or halfforgotten truths that he would bring before us. He is symbolised in the Scriptures both as the fire that refines and as the dove that soothes. By his inspiration we are given those words for which we would otherwise be at a loss, but by the same inspiration we can exercise the precious gift of silence.

Yes, we can use different colours in our churches, because their variety witnesses to the manifold nature of the Spirit and the manifold gifts that he bestows. Yet all point to the one basic truth — that God is real, present, living, immediate, here. That is what it means to believe in the Holy Spirit.

It means something else as well — something that we can (as people occasionally say of sermons) 'take away with us'. The Holy Spirit in his manifold activity is equal to the manifold needs of men and women. Perhaps there are some of you here who don't know how you are going to cope with the next bit of your life. Perhaps it is the demands of your work, or the fact that you don't have any; perhaps it is your own loneliness or fear, or the pressures put upon you by someone close to you. For all this, God promises what you need; turn to him and you will have the reserves of patience, strength, wisdom or endurance that you need. They may not come dramatically, and they may seem to be missing sometimes; but be patient — we are human, and we are living on earth! christ has promised his Spirit to all who follow him, and that promise he will fulfil.

The Holy Spirit is adequate to the needs of which you are conscious — but also to those of which you are not. For it is the function of the Spirit to open you to God, to open you to his world and the people in it — and that can mean that we're forced out of the grooves of convention or self-centredness. And that can be like letting the fresh air into some stale and musty room.

Praise be to the God who lives and gives us life!

TRINITY SUNDAY

The New Lectionary has indeed provided us with new lessons for the Eucharist on this day. No longer do we read that passage from Revelation that spoke of the 'sea of glass' and inspired Heber's hymn for this day. Nor do we read the story of Nicodemus and of what it means to be 'born again'. Instead we have passages from the letter to the Ephesians and the Gospel of St John both of which mention all three persons of the Trinity. Such passages hardly explain or describe a doctrine, not yet formulated; but they seem to assume it.

There is, however, one constant in the lessons for this day — and that is the first eight verses of Isaiah 6. It is easy to see why it was chosen — in former times as well as our own. In it we find the great anthem 'Holy, holy, holy is the Lord of hosts; the whole earth is full of his glory.' The anthem is echoed in the book of Revelation, and sung by Christians of many traditions and many centuries at the heart of the Eucharist. An Old Testament prophet who acknowledges the thrice-holy God seems to have come somewhere near that idea of Trinity of which he had never heard. So the passage remains an accepted part of our worship on this day.

But I want us to think of the preamble to all this — of that little detail with which the great chapter begins. 'In the year that King Uzziah died . . . '. Who does the prophet bother to tell us that? Well, the biblical writers in general are careful to establish dates and places, and usually they contribute in some way to the significance of the story they want us to hear. The biblical writers are not like people describing some illness who take ages to decide on which particular day the doctor did eventually come. For a prophet, when and how things happened actually matters. These things affect what happened. So why does Isaiah tell us that it was all 'In the year that King Uzziah died'?

Uzziah had a long reign — in many ways a glorious reign. You can read of his successes and his achievements in the second book of Chronicles. You can read also of his pride and his downfall, and the leprosy that made him as good as dead whilst he still lived. Isaiah had been subject and courtier of this king. And as J.E. Fison once wrote, 'It is at the moment when Yahweh's earthly representative has failed to reflect his glory that glory breaks forth in the very place of his representative's trespass.'

It is therefore as people fail and systems fail that Isaiah has his great vision. He sees that *the* King is the Lord, not Uzziah. He sees what is meant by true worship and obedience to this King.

Trinity Sunday points us to the greatness and the wonder and the other-ness of God. Often we fail to worship him because we put other things where he alone has a right to reign. We do this with people. It is hard not to do so when there are those whom you love very dearly. But once you *idolise* people, you find they have feet of clay. The Cavalier poet, Lovelace wrote:

> I could not love thee dear, so much
> Loved I not honour more.

And in the same century, the Scottish reformer, Andrew Melville preached before James VI, 'There are two kings and two kingdoms in the realm. King James, Head of the State, and King Jesus, Head of the Church. In his kingdom, James is not a lord, but a member.' Such quotations are not meant to detract from love to those to whom we are bound, or from respect to those in authority. Indeed, through such love we can come to understand the love of God, and through earthly obedience come to understand obedience to the Lord. Yet Isaiah's moment of truth came when he saw the mortality of a once-honoured King, and sometimes it is through such traumas that we understand that One only is worthy of our worship.

And we can enthrone systems where God alone has a right to reign. Again, the round of praise and offering in the Temple taught Isaiah something of worship; but the things of the Temple paled into insignificance when the glory of the Lord was revealed in it. The structures and activities and services of the Church are part of the discipline of our own life, but they can become idols, substitutes for worship and obedience to God himself. I do not wish to deny the importance of formulating for the minds of men the great doctrine of the Trinity or to under-rate the agonising of the Church which led to its formulation. But it is not a mathematical conundrum to be 'worked out'. It is instead a means whereby we are drawn to the worship and service of God in all its fulness and majesty. Perhaps the greatest hymn for this festival is that which Isaac Watts offered as a doxology for use at the Lord's Supper. And its last verse runs:

Almighty God, to Thee
Be endless honours done,
The undivided Three
And the Mysterious One.
Where reason fails
With all her powers,
There faith prevails
And love adores.

Trinity Sunday raises us up to God in all his excellence and other-ness. And on this day we read the story of Isaiah, which is not so much about the good and the bad as about the best and the second best. Without his vision and all that followed, he might have led a decent, worthy and useful life. Only because of it does he become one of the greatest of Christ's forerunners.

ALL SAINTS

2 Corinthians 4. 7 We are no better than pots of earthenware to contain this treasure.

We don't live in an age of heroes. People sometimes complain that there don't seem to be great leaders around today — in Church, or State, or anywhere else. It's not clear what we would do with them if we had them. First, they don't fit well into government by endless committees. Secondly, the media find out the weak spots in anybody; one wonders how John Wesley or Mr. Gladstone would have fared if they had been constantly on the television screen.

In any case, we don't seem to like leaders. It may have been Cromwell's men who knocked down the statues at the east and of the Lady Chapel in Gloucester Cathedral. But we do the same thing with the heroes of the past. Our age likes to discover that people are no better than they ought to be. If you write a biography about someone without mentioning any sexual peculiarities, it is not likely to sell!

But in one way, our refusal to put people on pedestals is in accordance with what Paul is saying in my text: 'we are no better than pots of earthenware to contain this treasure'. When God calls men and women to his service, he doesn't wait until he finds someone perfect. Think of the chosen race. We read in page after page of the Old Testament how that people disobeyed him, turned from him, got it all wrong, became obstinate and self-willed. Yet this people, above all races, understood the dealings of God with men. He chose Jacob — who was mean and sly and deceitful — yet had within him the drive and the vision that were needed. If I may put it this way, God has always taken enormous risks — with the peasant girl chosen to be the mother of his Son, or with Paul who could lose his temper and fall into despair, yet had within him the heart of the matter.

I'd like to bring this close to home. Where did you get your faith from? You got it from men and women who lived by it, witnessed to it and passed it on for twenty centuries. But more directly, you got it again from people — from clergy in your parishes; from teachers in school or in church; from parents; from someone who bothered about you in days of adolescence, someone to whom you could turn; from a friend who set you right when you were on the wrong track. Maybe, too, you were influenced by the lives and writings of Christians who lived in past centuries. It was through *people* that God made himself known to you.

And they were none of them perfect people. They had their limitations, their blind spots, their sins. Sometimes their actions seemed to belie the faith for which they stood. How could Chistians in the eighteenth century be so blind to the evils of the slave trade? How could some Victorian churchmen readily accept an order of society that permitted such massive inequalities of wealth? How could a twentieth century bishop, known in his diocese and beyond as one of the kindest of men, be such a defender of the death penalty?

Yet these people's imperfections do not deny the validity of the things they taught. As Fr Harry Williams has said, 'Saintliness doesn't mean all-round perfection.' So don't let a person's bad qualities blind you to those good qualities in him — which are of Christ. We are no better than pots of earthenware to contain this treasure.

I asked you one question just now — 'How did you get your faith?' Now I ask another 'How is that faith going to be passed on?' The answer is surely the same: through people. It can be passed on through those of you who are parents; through those of you who are able to make something of your role as godparents; through those of you who teach; through those of you who are caring about people in your neighbourhood, through those of you who are trying to help in bad times; through those of you who are helping to change the character of the society in which we live.

Remember once again — God does not wait for perfect people when he wants men and women to serve him. The clergy aren't perfect: I know this because I'm one of them. But as Lord Soper once said about the selection of ministers 'We've only got the laity to choose from'. In the same chapter from which my text is taken we find the words — 'It is not ourselves we proclaim, but Christ Jesus our Lord'. It has been said that no true preacher of the gospel wants people to say of himself, 'He's a wonderful man', but rather, 'Christ is a wonderful Saviour'. All this applies to congregations as well as to preachers, to laity as well as to clergy. We do not want people to think of our local church as *simply* a jolly and helpful club (though it's no bad thing if they do think of it in this way!); we want them to know the Lord of the Church. An old Evangelical hymn ran:

> May his beauty rest upon me
> As I seek the lost to win,
> And may they forget the channel,
> Seeing only Him.

In fact, the less we think about ourselves as we seek to commend our faith, the better; in his small book *Your Faith* David Edwards notes that the really attractive person is often the person most interested in other people.

Of course none of us is good enough or clever enough for the task of communicating the Gospel. But then, no one ever has been. Our faith has come to us through imperfect people — and will be passed on by imperfect people. We are no better than pots of earthenware to contain this treasure. But it is not ourselves we proclaim, but Christ Jesus as Lord.

SPECIAL GROUPS

1 Nurses

Philippians 3. 10,11. All I care for is to know Christ, to experience the power of his resurrection, and to share his sufferings, in growing conformity with his death, if only I may finally arrive at the resurrection from the dead.

In my first parish the Vicar was a Hospital Chaplain, in two small hospitals, and the plan was that I should help him in them, and gradually take over the work from him. Before I was ordained, the Bishop said to me 'My boy' (Bishops spoke to ordinands in that way in those days!) — 'My boy, if you want to know about grace and resurrection and the Holy Spirit, spend all the time you can in those hospitals.' I thought it a strange thing to say at the time. For I had just finished my theological course. I had read books and written essays on grace and resurrection and the Holy Spirit. I had passed exams on such subjects as these.

But after working in the hospitals for a few months, I began to see what he meant. When St Paul spoke of 'knowing' Christ, he did not just mean knowing about him. He meant a personal experience of Christ. There is a world of difference between understanding the things of the Christian faith with our minds and actually experiencing them in our lives. In the Old Testament the word 'know' is used to denote the most intimate and deepest relationships of life. It is in this sense that Paul uses the word. And something of this I was to experience in my two hospitals. It was not that the staff or the patients talked often of grace and resurrection and the Holy Spirit. It was that these things became real in the compassion, the caring and the courage of hospital life. I do not wish to paint too rosy a picture of it — especially as it is some distance away; nor do I think that, as a chaplain, I went around with particularly blinkered eyes. But it is true that I began to know something of grace and resurrection and the Holy Spirit through my work in those years.

Some of us have direct contact with hospitals and work in them. Others are less directly involved, and others have retired. And in any case our job is not our whole life. But for all of us who are Christians, one object of our discipleship is to know Christ in this intimate and personal way. This is first made clear in baptism. The plunging into water represents our identification with Christ's death, our coming out of it represents our identification with his resurrection. When anyone is baptised — either as an adult or an infant — the prayer of the Church is that he will experience for himself what has been enacted symbolically in the sacrament.

We are to share his sufferings. This means more than accepting

65

with courage the sorrows or the pains that come our way. It means a willingness to take on board some of the sorrows and pains of this world. There are opportunities enough for this in hospital. Of course, those who work there tread a bit of a tight-rope in this matter. A degree of professional detachment is necessary in order to get the work done at all, yet a total hardness will mean that it is not done as well as it could be. What is true of specialised work in hospitals is true of us all. We cannot sympathise with everybody at every moment. Those whose work is primarily pastoral know that they can take on only a limited number of difficult 'cases' at a time — for strength, patience and attention are needed. But we can all take *some* sorrows and enter into them with our time, our imagination and our prayers. It is this *voluntary* acceptance of sorrow or pain that is surely meant by sharing Christ's sorrows.

But we are to share also in the power of His resurrection. Suffering is evident; resurrection is not. Yet it is again not just something that we are to read about or to try to understand with our minds. It is something that we are to experience for ourselves. The first disciples knew this in two ways. First, they believed that the risen Christ was still with them. The Gospels end with a series of 'appearances' or 'experiences' of the risen Christ — and when these came to an end they left the conviction that he was still with them, that the power that flowed through him was still flowing through them. Secondly, they knew that death was not the end for them because it had not been the end for him. They believed that love was stronger than death, and that the finality of death had now been conquered.

It seems much easier for people who lived in those times, but how do we now experience the power of Christ's resurrection? A writer who has helped people enormously during the last decade is Fr Harry Williams of the Community of the Resurrection in a book called *True Resurrection*. He cites a number of people who have experienced the power of resurrection in their lives, though they might never have thought of putting it in this way. He talks of the scientist whose favourite theory is shown to be false, and whose work lies in ruins; but then gradually and patiently he starts to wrestle with his problem again. He speaks of the married couple whose love seems quite dead; but gradually again they find a new relationship, different from the old one 'but deeper, more stable, more satisfying, with a new quality of life . . .'. He speaks of illness and bereavement — familiar themes to us, but helping us to see that we have experienced resurrection on the wards and in the waiting rooms of our hospitals.

There is one thing more. You may have noticed in the text that Paul did not speak of this knowledge of Christ as something he had finally acquired. He spoke of it as an on-going process. What is true of any human relationship is true of our relationship with Christ. It is in the 'changing scenes of life' that we discover different aspects of this truth, and know it in different ways. This knowledge then is involved with process, with pilgrimage. And it has a promise, a goal; that one day, in the day of the Lord, we shall know, even as we are known by him.

SPECIAL GROUPS

2 Teachers

Philippians 3. 1–14

We were privileged to read that chapter from St Paul's writings. We are privileged to have that chapter in the Bible. It tells us things about the man that we would not otherwise know. Elsewhere in the New Testament we have at least three accounts of his conversion. Many pages are devoted to his adventures, to the trials he endured and the perils that he faced. In the letter to the Romans we have such a systematic account of his thoughts that C.H. Dodd called it 'the Gospel according to Paul'. But here in the letter to Philippi, as perhaps nowhere else, we have a clue about what his faith meant to him personally — a potted spiritual autobiography.

And I think it shows us two things about him — that he was a man of convictions, and that he was a man of open-ness. That he was a man of convictions becomes obvious when you turn to any of his letters. But C.S. Lewis once said, 'you never know how much you believe anything until its truth or falsehood becomes a matter of life and death to you.'

And in the passage that we read, those convictions and their cost are set out with a starkness that we don't see elsewhere. Remember that Paul was one of the first to walk by faith and not by sight (to use his own phrase). We have no record that he ever saw Jesus in the flesh. All that he believed about the unique character of the Lord, about his atoning death, about the resurrection — all came from faith in these things.

But he was also a man of open-ness. That is clearer in this chapter than anywhere else in his writings. He realised that there was an end to be reached; and he realised that he had a long way to go in order to reach it. This is not the conventional talk of those who say that they learn more from their pupils than they ever teach them. This is not the fashion of the last decade which has sought to blur all distinctions between teacher and student. Paul was a teacher, and he accepted his role as a teacher. But he still has to learn. He presses on 'hoping to take hold of that for which Christ once took hold of me.' If the language is obscure, the though does not encourage precision. But there is a maturity to be achieved. There is a process ahead as well as behind. Cerebral knowledge may be implied; non-cerebral is certainly stated. For when Paul speaks of knowing Christ and the power of his resurrection, he is using the most intimate word of relationship in his vocabulary. He is speaking of something that must motivate his whole being.

After spending so long on these two characteristics of Paul, it will be obvious that I want to apply them to teachers. The reference is in fact wider; for surely, these are characteristics that we want to develop in students, characteristics that we would like to see in the Christian community as a whole. But let's see what they mean for the more specialised part of the congregation.

First, then, we are to be men and women of convictions. We shall never cut any ice as Christian teachers unless we are such, and known to be such. I don't think we can easily particularise about the relationship of this to the subjects that we teach. I have no idea how you would teach mathematics Christianly. But we are people; and for that reason, are of more interest to those whom we teach than we always realise. We ought not, as occasion arises, to be afraid of saying what we believe and why. The first Christians were told to be ready to give a reason for the hope that was in them — yet to do so with fear and trembling. The fear and trembling are necessary because of the magnitude of that which holds us. The Christian faith cannot be encapsulated in words, and may well be vitiated by our characters. But a declaration of belief given by a Christian teacher is emphatically not indoctrination.

But we are also to be men and women of open-ness. This aspect of our calling has not always been given the emphasis it deserves. Built into Christianity is the doctrine of the Holy Spirit and the belief that he will guide us into all truth. What has passed for orthodox Christianity has often to all intents and purposes been binitarianism — which has affirmed the first two persons of the Trinity, but ignored the third. As a result, the Church has often given the impression that all there is to know about God has been made known; and that all we have to do is to guard it, keep it intact and pass it on. But the doctrine of the Holy Spirit means there is more to be revealed, more to be learned. In the celebrated phrase of the Pilgrim Fathers 'the Lord hath yet more light and truth to pour upon his word'. If this also becomes part of us it will be something that we shall want to pass on — that Christianity does not provide all the answers at a sitting or even during a course, that the Christian pilgrimage is a pursuit of truth as well as of holiness and love. And we shall want to affirm that although it is part of our calling to give our *minds* to understand God's ways, we have also to learn what it means to live with mystery.

Convictions and open-ness: I have tried to show that they are complementary, for I believe that they are. How tragic that they have sometimes been seen in antithesis; that strong beliefs have meant a closed mind, and that open-ness has involved little commitment. Perhaps the theological debates of the last two decades have set the two against each other. But this need not, and should not be so. It was not so for Paul who, although convinced of the truth of Christ said he had to press on to *know* it.

SPECIAL GROUPS

3 Mothers

St Luke 10. 42 One thing is necessary

The evangelist's sympathy seems to lie with Mary, and many of us warm instinctively to Martha. And the Penguin commentary on St Luke's Gospel rightly says that few stories have been so consistently mishandled as this one.

Let's be quite clear that neither the evangelist nor Jesus sought to undervalue Martha. She is a strong character. When she makes an appearance in St John's Gospel after the death of her brother, it is to ask probing questions about the resurrection. Moreover, Jesus appreciated hospitality. Maybe he had been brought up in a home like this. Maybe he saw the steam rising, and smelt something burning, and knew the effort that had gone into it all. The story is told to defend Mary, not to denigrate Martha. But it has been misunderstood. In the Middle Ages, it was used to justify the superiority of the contemplative life over the active. In more modern devotion, Mary has been seen as the spiritual one who understood the things of the Kingdom which her sister missed. And most people miss now the humour of the story, and the half-bantering way in which Jesus spoke.

But let's look at the text with which the story ends. The 'one thing needful' is capable of more than one interpretation; there are at least three. Now if you think that the preacher is making a simple story difficult, please don't switch off. For each of the three possible meanings has value for us, and one of them may be the message that you need to hear.

The first possibility is that when Jesus said 'One thing is necessary' he meant 'necessary for us all' and referred to one dish on the menu. Martha was, in the choice phrase of the Authorised Version 'cumbered about much serving' and one simple dish would have sufficed. We are always being told that we eat too much, and that we eat too richly. There is no virtue in dull meals, and surely good cooking is to the glory of God. But a certain simplicity in our living would hurt none of us. There are those who can't entertain unless they do so on a lavish scale. 'Whenever we have visitors, mother always thinks the place ought to be like a hotel' was the reply of a lady asked to put up a student for a weekend. There is a place for spontaneous, homely, simple hospitality.

But there is certainly a place for *hospitality* as such in this not very hospitable age. A retired clergyman agreed to go and take duty for three Sundays in a parish some miles away from his home. The services were at 8.00 and 10.00, and he imagined someone would offer him breakfast. But it was not to be; on the first Sunday after the 8 o'clock service the churchwarden said 'See you later then'. And on subsequent Sundays the priest took a flask and sandwiches. In some parishes — during a vacancy — it is no one's business to think of these things. But it is the kind of thing mothers think of, and the kind of thing that the Mothers' Union ought to think of. Martha overdid hospitality, but she certainly set an example of it. The Mothers' Union could set an example of hospitality (perhaps most of all to lonely people) in the world of today.

Secondly, when Jesus said 'One thing is necessary', he may have meant, 'One thing is necessary for me'. People react differently after a busy day. Some just want to be quiet, some want to talk. Perhaps Mary, by her willingness to listen, provided the one thing he most needed. Most of us, whether married or single, need someone who will listen to us. All of us who have had good homes remember that mother was the one who always had time to listen to us. Those of you who have young or growing children don't need me to remind you of how important it is that your children should find you available. Those of you with children who are grown up or gone away can still find a ministry along these lines. I cannot be the only priest to testify to what it has meant to have, in a variety of parishes, women who have been in the biblical phrase 'a mother in Israel' — women to whom I could turn, whose discretion could be relied upon, who sometimes helped me to see things from a different angle. Such people ought to be part of our normal living, and maybe Mothers' Union members could take a lead here.

In our society, an organisation like the Samaritans has shown us how the art of listening provides a form of healing to the troubled. People with huge problems can sometimes come near to coping with them — if they have someone who will listen. It's not easy work; it needs patience, concentration, time. But as we look at this story from the Gospels, we are reminded that our Lord may have needed someone to talk to, and that someone may have been Mary. And he has told us that whatever we do for his brothers and sisters in this world, we do for him.

The third explanation is the most conventional. When Jesus said 'One thing is necessary', he meant, 'One thing is necessary for you'. There is, as we have seen, no condemnation of Martha's activity. The little story in the Gospel directly follows the parable of the Good Samaritan where the hero is the man who acts out what he believes. Jesus needed his supper, and Martha gave it to him. But with all her energy, she needed sometimes to do what her sister had done — to be still and listen. It is the need of us all. The Sabbath may have had its origins as much in the need of wholeness for the body as holiness for the soul — though the Jews would not have recognised the distinction. There must be listening as well as talking, stillness as well as activity. It has been said that the Society of Friends is a standing refutation of the common image of Christianity — a parson talking! Mothers are busy people, and always on demand; but here again could not the Mothers' Union witness to the priority of waiting upon God? The busier you are, the more important it is.

The story was told to defend Mary, not to denigrate Martha. We need both. The Church always needs variety. In an early morning radio talk, Dr John Newton compared the image of the present Pope with the last Archbishop of Canterbury, and said that the Church needed the gifts of both. Certainly it needs its Marthas and its Marys; but most of us need a bit of both.

SPECIAL GROUPS

4 Minorities

Psalm 118. 6 The Lord is on my side, I will not fear: what can man do to me?

I don't know whether you find the confidence of the psalmist inspiring or embarrassing. Although I've gone back to the Old Testament for my text, it expresses a sentiment that has been known throughout Christian history. It has supported the warrior, the crusader, the confessor and the martyr. Many of the victories won by minorities over the centuries might never have been achieved without the confidence of this text.

But it has also been the sort of text that has fired the fanatic, the persecutor and the zealot. All sorts of people have claimed special insight into God's purposes, and special protection from him for courses of action that don't seem to us to be Christian. And between examples of heroic sanctity and examples of appalling bigotry, there are grey areas. We are told that when William of Orange landed at Torbay, the debarkation of the troops was treated as a religious exercise; and before they pitched camp, they gathered on the beach to sing Psalm 118.

The difficulty that many of us feel about claiming divine protection arises from two related ideas that belong to our generation. First, we wonder whether God does take sides in quite that crude way that Old Testament writers declared, and some people in the two World Wars believed. Secondly, the issues which divide people seem so much more complex than many of our forefathers were able or willing to admit. Life for most of us is not a matter of black or white; it looks much more like different shades of grey.

Having said all this, it looks as if I were wasting your time and mine in inviting you to consider such a text. Well, I don't think this is a waste of time, and that's why I'm continuing my sermon. I think the psalmist has something important to say to us in two areas: the first concerns what we are, and the second what we do.

I believe that the first thing that Christianity has to say to us is that we are loved and accepted by God, and that we are of infinite worth in his sight. And I think that the realisation of this, the recollection of 'amazing grace' is always a source of wonder and of joy. It is parallel to the human experience of being loved and wanted by another person. That experience can lead us to the love of God. But sometimes God's love is most real to us when we have been let down or rejected by other people, when we feel on our own. We are creatures made for loving and being loved — however badly we seem to do either. But to know that the love we experience so fragmentarily is at the heart of all things — in a God whose supreme revelation is in Jesus Christ, this is to know that we matter. This is not something that we take in once and for all. It is renewed for us in all sorts of ways. It is as fresh and good as lovers' meetings.

The eighteenth century poet, William Cowper, told a story of a bullying he endured in his very unhappy school days, 'I well remember being afraid to lift my eyes upon him higher than his knees; and so I knew him better by his shoe-buckles than by any other part of his dress.' Yet as he sat on a bench in the schoolroom fearing the coming of his tormentor, he found in our text, 'A degree of trust and confidence in God that would have been no disgrace to a much more experienced Christian.' And, in later life, during the recoveries from many bouts of mental illness, it was this Psalm that he often quoted.

I mention Cowper's experience, because it is almost literally that of suffering Christians in many parts of the world today, and because metaphorically, it is the kind of thing that we have to face up to. Translate it into some situation of your own. But know that the Lord is on your side. You matter to him. Let that thought rise above all the things that degrade and dehumanise us.

The psalmist speaks of what we are. He speaks also of what we do. The congregation includes minorities. Some of you are supporting causes that are unpopular in the world and unfashionable in the Church. You are doing this because of your Christian convictions. This is what discipleship involves for you. You will not expect me to say that God is on the side of all these causes. God does not endorse all our blank cheques. In some things you may be mistaken; in some things you may be right.

We have been told some of the things that God does support. It is made clear in one Gospel passage by which we can never be unmoved, 'Lord, when was it that we saw you hungry and fed you, or thirsty and gave you drink, a stranger and took you home, naked and clothed you? When did we see you in prison and come to visit you?'

All works that are on the side of mercy and compassion, all causes that really seek the wholeness of human beings, these belong to the Kingdom of God. We must ask of the causes we support the degree in which they are doing that. And we must know that when they are, then we are on the winning side because the Lord is on our side. At the heart of our faith is the conviction that suffering, crucified love is victorious. This is what remains when the powers and dominions of this world have crumbled into dust. This is the one thing that is indestructible.

I have spoken to you of the confidence that belongs to his people. I do not speak of churches and organisations that bear his name, but of those which bear his character. Many have come in his name who do not do his will. Many more will come. But where men and women are fulfilling his will, the Lord is on their side.

SPECIAL OCCASIONS

1 Choir Festival

It was an old-fashioned Evensong with Tallis' Festal Responses and the Cathedral Psalter. There were but two old ladies in the choir, but over a hundred people in the congregation. Most of them sat down to a beautifully-devised supper in the village hall, which was part of the Harvest Thanksgiving celebrations. After supper came an entertainment — led by a group of young gospel singers. Some people looked a bit surprised, for, after all they had

had their religion, and now they were having their entertainment. The leader asked the audience how many knew 'Burdens are lifted at Calvary'. Hardly anyone did — it wasn't the kind of thing you find in *Ancient and Modern*. But after one verse, the whole hall was singing.

Those young people were the latest in a long line. Once people have found Christianity true for themselves, they want to sing about it. The Reformation came marching in to Lutheran chorales; the eighteenth century revival to Wesley's hymns. The more reserved Tractarians translated ancient Greek and Latin hymns and brought them to life again. The modern charismatic movement has had its own style of song. What has been true of most forms of Christian revival was certainly true of the beginnings of Christianity. And that brings us to our text: Ephesians 5. 19. 'Speak to one another in psalms, hymns and songs; sing and make music in your hearts to the Lord.'

The early Church was a singing church. When Paul and Silas were put in prison, they sang hymns to keep up their spirits, and those of the other prisoners. When Pliny reported to his Emperor about the activities of the new sect, he said that one of its characteristics was to sing at dawn a hymn of praise to Christ as God. What sort of things did the first Christians sing?

Our text tells us that they sang psalms. The praises of Israel took on a new meaning. In our own day, we can take the songs of our forefathers (or some of them) and discover in them reality and power for ourselves. But the first Christians also sang hymns. They devised their own forms of praise. In various parts of the New Testament, we find fragments of the hymns that they sang. The letter to the Ephesians from which our text is taken has an example:

> Awake, sleeper, rise from the dead,
> And Christ will shine upon you.

Many commentators believe this to be a baptismal hymn. As we have seen, new forms of hymnody have attended every rival of Christianity. The first Christians also sang songs. The difference between hymns and songs is not very precise, but it is possible that there was a place for the more spontaneous song. The New Testament scholar, C. F. D. Moule, has described the worship of the early Church as 'anything but sedate'. And although 'Burdens are lifted at Calvary' is hardly likely to be chosen for a choir festival, yet there is a place within the Christian community for what has been called the 'disposable hymn'.

But this is a sermon, not a lecture, and I want to go on to ask what we are doing when we sing — what are the functions of music for choir and congregation in Christian worship?

You notice that our text began with the words 'Speak to one another . . . '. The songs of God's people are meant to build up God's people. When the choir sings by itself, it is not a form of entertainment; it is an act of worship and a means of worship. Sometimes their singing will draw out new meanings from the chosen texts; sometimes, the music itself will inspire us, purify us, strengthen us. The congregation can participate as much when it is listening as when it is singing, if the role of the choir is seen in that way. But when we all sing, it is an exercise in how to live harmoniously — working for one another, working one with the other. This is the way to sing together; and should the tune be unfamiliar, do not regard this as an appalling catastrophe, but as an opportunity to learn and be enlarged!

A second thing about our worship is implied by the text. It involves the whole of ourselves. The worship of the Reformation churches has often been described as too cerebral — the congregation is invited to use its ears and no more. In our century we have seen the growth of liturgical dance; clapping is no longer forbidden in church, though the present preacher has had it happen only once in the course of a sermon! The fact that we use our voices as well as our minds does witness to this truth; and as every singer knows, you make the best use of your voice when your body is in the right position.

But finally, we are to sing and make music in our hearts to the Lord. Our singing is not unrelated to our feelings and intentions. It is common to speak of worship, and music in worship, in terms of offering. I think it is more accurate to think of it in terms of response. We sing because of what God is and what he does. As so often, Charles Wesley puts it succinctly:

> My heart is full of Christ, and longs
> Its glorious matter to declare,
> Of Him I raise my loftier songs,
> I cannot from His praise forbear.

The songs of God's people are the songs of those whom he has redeemed.

SPECIAL OCCASIONS

2 Missionary Festival

Acts 28. 14 And so we came to Rome.

There are moments in life for which we cannot find words. Perhaps this was one for the writer of the Acts of the Apostles. When he comes to the climax of his great story, he has one bald, almost laconic little phrase — 'And so we came to Rome.'

But what a moment! The Acts of the Apostles opens with a promise of power for the first disciples. With that power — the power of the Holy Spirit — they would be able to preach the Gospel not only in Jerusalem and in Judaea, but in the uttermost parts of the earth. For them, the centre of it all was Rome. Paul, as we know, was proud of his citizenship of that great city. He wanted to go there. The fact that he ever got there was partly fortuitous. But what a moment!

Maybe you have walked along the Appian Way — looking by modern standards like a dusty narrow lane. Along this road travelled so many of the great. And when I stood there, I thought of Paul the prisoner passing that way. Yet he tells us that in comparison with the knowledge of his Lord, all else seemed garbage. And now came the chance to preach the Gospel in Rome. The uttermost ends of the earth had been reached.

Two thousand years later, we see that the dream of Paul and his friends has been partly fulfilled, partly shattered. Indeed Rome and its great Empire were Christianised; indeed, the Gospel has been carried to lands of which Paul had never heard. But in human terms we don't see the least likelihood of Christianity becoming the dominant world religion, much less the universal faith. We don't have to look beyond our own country to face up to this bit of realism. For here we see two facts. First, there is the well-known and widespread decline of the faith that was once an integral and accepted part of our culture. Secondly, this post-Christian land is now one of many faiths, and the mosque and the temple have become familiar to most of us.

What, then, is the missionary outlook for the Church? And how is it to be informed by the greatest of all missionary stories that we find in the Acts of the Apostles? Well, if we are to have any missionary sense at all, then we must first have a message. That message must be more than 'Come to church', more than a general idea that Christianity will lessen crime and do people good. These are secondary things. What is primary is the belief that something has been done for the world that alters its character, that something is being done that makes life different from what it would otherwise be. This is difficult to put into words that don't sound stale and conventional. But there are some who try. At a recent conference of the Hymn Society we sang a modern hymn which contained the couplet:

> Life is great if someone loves me
> Holds my hand and calls my name.

There is an experience here that most of us can latch on to. It's a human message. But the Gospel message is that God loves us, holds our hand and calls our name. That human love, often so fickle and frail, is a reflection of the divine love — which in the end is all that matters. The good news of the Gospel — that we are loved and wanted is one that can transform life, personal and corporate. If this is true then we have a message for today.

The early missionaries had not only a message. They had a goal. Their goal was the evengelisation of the world. That has been the impetus behind Christian mission right up to our time. But we have seen the unlikelihood that Christianity will become the universal faith. And perhaps that is not our goal. According to St Mark's Gospel, Jesus came preaching the Kingdom of God —

which means the rule of God over all things. The Christian Church, in its widest sense, is not the equivalent of the Kingdom of God; it is the instrument of the Kingdom of God. We do not fully understand what other instruments God has, or in what other ways he speaks to men and women. The founder of the Iona Community, George Macleod, once spoke of a missionary in a place where the only prayer was 'Allah is great'. The missionary never suggested that they should drop the word 'Allah' but he did ask them to try to say 'Allah is love'. I'm not saying that all religions are equally good; I don't believe that they are. I'm not saying that it doesn't matter what you believe; it does matter. I am saying that the Church is an instrument of the Kingdom of God, and that the goal to which we look is the fulfilment of that Kingdom.

As well as a goal and a message, the early Christians had a method. It took a long time to get to Rome. The story of how they got there is revealed in the Acts of the Apostles. But on the way, they made use of every opportunity of preaching the Gospel. The goal we have is long-term. It may never be fulfilled in time and space as we now understand them. It is, in any case, an act of God, not of men. But all of us can be involved in the process towards its achievement. This is the value of the activities of our Church, and of those with which we are identified outside. Earlier in the sermon, you may have wondered if they were worth while. They are worth while if their starting-point is the Christian message that God loves us, is redeeming us. And they are worth while if their finishing-point is the goal of God's Kingdom and its fulfilment. Without these things, all our organisations, and our churches themselves become no more than clubs for the like-minded. But they must be expressions of God's love, and intimations of his Kingdom. Our Church exists for nothing less than this, and certainly for nothing greater.

SPECIAL OCCASIONS

3 An Arts Festival

Psalm 29. 9 In his temple, all cry 'Glory'

I have always been embarrassed by the legal phrase 'act of God'. You know that it is applied to some explosion of nature which could not be foreseen or prevented. And it has always seemed to me to suggest some capricious, vengeful God who sometimes takes it into his head to send earthquake or volcano. Like many clergy, I've done my best to dissuade people from thinking that disaster or sickness are 'sent' to them.

Yet the psalmist sees God in the storm — in the very elements that seem destructive. The picture that he paints is lurid. The music that he composes is wild. The great storm that he describes breaks mighty trees, whirls the sands in the desert, causes animals in their terror to give premature birth to their young. Yet above this fearful scene, the Lord sits enthroned; in all this he still has care for his people; and despite all this confusion and devastation, all created things give glory to him.

This service comes at the end of your festival of arts, and I want to say, in the first place, that I believe it is the function of art to explore mystery. That is surely true of art in general; it is certainly true of art in the service of the Christian church, for it is also the function of theology. Now of course, Christian art must show us beauty; it must show us form, but it must also show us mystery. It must depict the awkward features of life as well as those which are attractive. And this means that it will have jagged edges or shattering discords. You have sometimes heard people say of a picture 'But I don't understand it' as though that dismissed the value of the picture for ever. But why should we expect always to understand it? Do we understand life? Again, when there is a national crisis, the prayers of the church are often for stability, and most of us can respond to that. But in the history of the human race, the voice of God has often been heard during great up-heavals, and some of man's finest achievements have been in

81

times of tumult. It is presumptuous to criticise so great and beautiful a work as Bach's St John Passion: but have you sometimes felt that in such a work, every splinter of the Cross has been carefully planed away?

What I believe the psalmist tells us is what men of vision have said in many centuries, and most certainly in our own: you musn't make your God too small, you musn't make your religion too neat. For this there are two reasons. First, that kind of religion will always let you down. Secondly, it leads to the ultimate idolatry of making God in our own image, making him no more than the sum total of our ambitious, ideals and prejudices. And he is so much more!

In art as in religion, there must be a place for mystery and wonder:

> God moves in a mysterious way
> His wonders to perform,
> He plants his footsteps in the sea
> And rides upon the storm.

So runs one of the most famous of the Olney Hymns whose bi-centenary we celebrated in 1979. Like the Psalm, it reminds us that he is still there — amid the devastation of our own plans, amid the very things that seem to thwart his own purpose. In the words of Charles Coulson who, in the middle of the century did so much to relate Christianity and Science, 'Either God is in the whole of Nature with no gaps, Or he is not there at all'.

But the Psalm does not end with the storm. The Lord not only sits enthroned above it, but

> 'The Lord will give strength to his people:
> the Lord will give his people the blessing of peace'.

The context of this verse warns us against what Dietrich Bonhoeffer called 'cheap grace'. It warns us against easy assurances, slick answers, the proclaiming of peace where there is no peace, the healing of wounds too lightly. The peace that God gives to his people is the peace which Jesus promised to his disciples. When they recognised him on Easter evening, his con-

ventional greeting 'Peace be with you' was given a new depth by
the words quoted earlier in St John's Gospel: 'My peace I give
you. Not as the world gives give I unto you.'

We are not offered the peace that comes from absence of
turmoil. It is rather the deep peace that can be held in the midst of
turmoil because we are assured that God's purposes are good, and
their final outcome certain. The great Indian leader, Mahatma
Ghandi put it this way: 'I am a man of peace. I believe in peace. . .
But I do not want the peace that you find in the grave. I want the
peace you find embedded in the human heart which is exposed to
the arrows of the whole world, but which is protected from all
harm by the power of Almighty God.'

Here is a much more difficult task for Christian art. It must
speak of purpose — but long-term purpose. It must speak of
peace — but the peace of God. Much of the art of Coventry
Cathedral has sought to do this; but it remains the most sensitive
task for artists and musicians, and one that can come only from a
depth of experience of this world and of faith in God.

Mystery and purpose: it is hard to combine the two. Yet only as
we hold both can we be protected from an attitude which is cynical
and despairing on the one hand, or shallow and facile on the other.
I would have art proclaim both, because our faith involves both.

SPECIAL OCCASIONS

4 Harvest Thanksgiving

I want to show you a picture, tell you a story, and then say
something that will, I hope, be to your advantage.

The picture is of a river valley, and the time is that of harvest. It
is a peaceful scene; for these are pre-tractor, pre-transistor days,
and maybe the only sound is that of people singing as they go
about their work. Now in the distance, there is the lowing of
cattle. There is nothing uncommon about that, but as it gets
nearer, so it sounds more urgent and somehow strange. And now
comes a remarkable sight. There is a cart drawn by two milch-

cows, and on the cart a box and what look like model animals. Behind the cart walk five foreigners — officials or civil servants by their dress. The people strain their eyes; they chatter excitedly to one another, and point to the box on the cart. And then quite suddenly and spontaneously there goes up a great shout of joy.

That is the picture. Perhaps you recognise it. If so, you know the story. You can find it is in the Bible, and if you know it, there is nothing quite so irritating as a preacher retelling a story in words that are not so good as the original. But just in case you haven't read the first book of Samuel very recently, here is a summary. The story concerns the box on the cart. This was the ark of the covenant — Israel's cherished possession. It may have contained the scroll of the Ten Commandments; it may have been a sort of throne on which the Lord was thought to sit in time of battle. Old Testament scholars have spent a lot of time on the Ark of the Covenant. Suffice it now to say that for the ancient people it symbolised the presence of God himself. The day came when the ark was captured in battle by Israel's traditional foes — the Philistines. They probably thought they had done well to get it, and that it would bring them luck. But it brought the reverse. It brought catastrophe upon catastrophe. First, their own god, Dagon, lay smashed in his temple; then came a plague of rats, then a plague of boils. The ark was sent from place to place, and finally the Philistines decided to get rid of it altogether. They took advice and acted upon it; and that is why it appeared in a river valley in a place called Beth-Shemesh on that harvest day. And that was the reason for the great shout of joy that went up from the wheat fields. The ark had come back — and the Lord seemed to have come back as well.

The text of the Bible is not clear about what happened next — except that the happy scene was marred in some way. One version says that the sons of Jeconiah did not rejoice — and disaster befell them. Another version says that curiosity overcame some people and they opened the box to see what they were not meant to see — again with disastrous consequences. Perhaps there is not too great a distinction between indifference and irreverence.

But there we will leave the story. It is the harvest season, and many preachers find themselves ploughing the fields and scattering for quite a few weeks. The harvest itself is a sign of God's presence amongst us, and the harvest thanksgiving services are a recognition of his presence. So as services are held in churches and halls and schools and pubs it is as though the ark of the covenant were being carried into our midst, for we are acknowledging the presence and the reality of God.

It is the gifts of a gracious God that we remember today. We have tokens of those gifts all around us. We are reminded of our daily bread, and the good things to eat that go with it. Through the beauty and colour of the flowers, we are reminded of the gifts by which our spirit is sustained. This is surely also a moment to let our imagination dwell on things which we normally take for granted — the comforts we enjoy, the hard work that other people do, the faithfulness of those who supply our needs. This service shows that these things are gifts — not rights — as we sometimes suppose. The harvest decorations speak of graciousness in the world as well as hard commerce. Above all, they point to the gifts of a gracious God.

But with the gifts of a gracious God, there are also the demands of a gracious God. I said it was possible that the Ark of the Covenant contained the Ten Commandments — the rules by which that ancient society was meant to order its life. So too, the recognition of the presence of God amongst us now means a recognition of his claims upon us. We are told that we have God's gifts on trust. We are to develop the earth without exploiting it, for it is the Lord's. We are to do all we can to ensure that the harvests of this world are properly shared. It is common for gifts to be taken to the elderly and sick — as tokens that such people are not forgotten by the congregation, that they are still part of us when they cannot be with us. But 'neighbour' means so much more in this global village. This is something we must bear in mind throughout the year, and press at whatever level we can, for a more just distribution of our resources. But at this service, if you really want to say 'thank you', to respond to this token of God's presence, the most practical thing you can do is to give a donation to one of the agencies for famine relief and development in poor countries.

The story that I told had a sad ending — either of indifference or irreverence. May the story or our lives be of those who joyfully recognise the presence of God, and in accepting him as Lord, find our true selves.

SPECIAL OCCASIONS

5 Remembrance Sunday

We are a most varied congregation, yet united in one thing — remembrance. Some of you — not many now — were in the first World War, and you think of the comrades of those far-off years. Many of you fought and suffered in the second World War, and you are still conscious of gaps that can never be filled, of might-have-beens that still haunt your lives. And I do not forget that most people here remember neither war. What I want to say applies as much to you as to the rest; first, because you have inherited the world left by those wars, and secondly because although you do not share the memories of the older people, you still have memories. And the question that I want to ask you all is simply this: what do we do with our memories?

I take it that we all see some value in remembrance, and that is why we are here. And the fact is that we cannot cut ourselves off from the past — either as individuals or as a society. Part of what I am, part of what you are depends upon heredity and the influences of early childhood. When psychiatrists try to heal the mind, they must probe into the past. Societies are what they are because of what happened; as I have said, we are all inheritors of the two world wars. It was John XXIII who really changed the image of Papacy in our century, and with it, that of the Church which he represented. Yet he once said, 'Do not be like those people who think they are inaugurating a new era; as if before they came along, there had been nothing but emptiness or chaos. Before we came, there were our parents, and they were the latest links of a long and sacred chain. . . We should still be very wretched indeed, and hardly out of the phase of barbarism, if the civilisation of past centuries had not seen to our baptism.'

But what are we to do with our memories? You can do two things. And you can find both in the pages of the Bible. First, you can live in the past. You can become the prisoner of nostalgia. Turn up those parts of the Old Testament which deal with the deliverance of Israel from Egypt, and you will see that once things got difficult, the people looked back, and wished they were back. They forgot the oppression of body and spirit which they had endured, and thought only of the security.

For memory plays strange tricks. People talk about 'the Dunkirk spirit' forgetting what Dunkirk was really like. People think of the courage and heroism that undoubtedly blossomed in time of war, and forget the black market and the dodges and the lies that it engendered. Church people look back on full churches, forgetting that they were full only on certain occasions, and that some people were there only because it paid them to be. We all tend to remember only what we want to remember — investing the past with a rosy glow that it never had.

Yet all of us have memories that are genuinely good, lovely memories. Who is to grudge them to us if they give comfort to us in bad times? Who indeed? But isn't there a kind of remembering, of looking back that saps our vitality? That is what I am warning you about, what I think the Bible is warning us about. Another famous Old Testament story is paralleled in the world's litera-ture. Lot's wife looked back on the smouldering ruins of Sodom, and was turned to a pillar of salt.

That's one use of memory. But there is another. There is that kind of remembering that lies at the heart of Christian worship — and indeed of Jewish worship as well. When Jews celebrate the great events of their history like the deliverance from Egypt, it is to affirm that God is still like that, a 'delivering-out-of-Egypt-sort-of-God', as an Oxford lecturer used to put it. When Christians celebrate the birth, death and resurrection of Jesus, it is not in order to escape from the realities of this world into one that seems less complicated. It is to affirm that the God who did these things is doing them now — still identified with us, still suffering for us, still triumphant over that suffering. We look back to the past, we trace the story of God's dealings with his people in order to know how he is dealing with us now. History has been called 'God's roaring loom'; we would be foolish if we tried to find in it too neat a pattern with no raw edges, but we would be blind if we did not see in it the activity of God who is for ever visiting and redeeming his people.

Try to apply this to your own memories. Some bring pain, some pleasure, but most a mixture of the two. Through them God speaks to you, and tells you that just as he led you to know love or to endure suffering, so he will now. For he is the same God. Therefore use memory — not as a retreat from life, not as a false yardstick with which to compare present ills, but as a source of power. The God whom we worship is a delivering God. There is still a 'promised land' for ourselves as individuals, and for the world society to which we belong. What he asks is the love and obedience that will enable him to lead us to it.

CHARACTER IN CHANGING TIMES

1 Eli

He never did anyone any harm — yet he and his household were damned. Such was the fate of Eli, priest and judge of Israel. It sounds a hard fate on the evidence of those chapters which record his story.

You will be better able to follow this course of sermons if you read the chapters on which they are based — the first ten or so in the first book of Samuel. We are thinking of character in changing times, and we are going to look at the ways in which three men responded to change. The changes they had to face were very different from those which confront us; but their response can help us to look critically at our own.

What kind of change did they face? The book of Judges ends with a famous and quotable verse:

> 'In those days there was no king in Israel, and every
> man did what was right in his own eyes.'

The text ushers in the books of Samuel and Kings. Israel was becoming a nation rather than a group of nomadic tribes. You can find a parallel with the end of the Middle Ages in our own country; under the great Tudor dynasty it became a nation in a sense that it had not been before. The era of Renaissance and Reformation was a stirring one in which to live; so were the years described in the first book of Samuel — the times of Eli, Samuel and Saul.

So to Eli: he seems a kindly, if rather dim old man. In the jargon of the last few years, we should say that he needed some sensitivity-training. At the opening of the story, he completely misunderstood the longing of the woman who stood in the sanctuary; perhaps he wasn't too accustomed to find people praying there. Once he found out, his attitude changed; for he was a kindly man. He recognised Samuel's gifts and encouraged them. He showed no envy of someone abler than himself, and he did not resent the fact that the word of God was revealed to a young layman rather than to himself, the accredited priest of Israel. Those were real virtues; and they are always virtues when they are found amongst ageing ecclesiastics who sometimes behave otherwise!

But there was another side to Eli. Basically, he was a weak man. He was in authority, but he wouldn't shoulder responsibility and the two must always go together. He had two sons who really ran the sanctuary; there is more than a hint of corruption about them, and certainly a suggestion that they lined their own pockets in the course of the job. Eli rebuked them — but no more. We sympathise a bit. Maybe you've got sons who go a way that is not yours, and you can't do much about it. But remember the power of the father in Old Testament times; more important still, remember the position of trust in which Eli was placed. Think of the influence that he could have exerted.

His story reminds us that negative virtues are not enough for the service of God. And Eli's virtues were mostly negative. A great nineteenth century preacher, F.W. Robertson, after making out as good a case for Eli as he could, went on to say, 'He was forgiving to his sons, because he was unable to feel the viciousness of sin; free from jealousy because he had no keen affections; submissive, because he was too indolent to feel rebellious. Before we praise a man for his excellencies, we must be sure that they do not arise from his defects.'

Those again are harsh words on the evidence of the chapters, but in those chapters we see Eli and his house doomed. The set-up which he represented had become an irrelevance to the times in which he lived, an incubus in the new age that was dawning.

To whom then does Eli speak? I think he speaks to the old in spirit. Eli was an old man, and, as the arteries harden, we feel less inclined for battle, more inclined to let things ride. Nevertheless, there is a sense in which age is relative, and some people of seventy are younger in outlook than some who are seventeen. That is why he speaks to the old in spirit.

And the old in spirit can respond to change in three ways. The first is by retreating from it — by shutting themselves off from the world in which things happen, by immersing themselves in their own families or religion or hobbies, as the case may be. Secondly, they can suppose it is enough to preserve a negative morality for themselves, that 'never doing anybody any harm' is a recommendation for the Kingdom of God. Thirdly, they can think they have a made contribution to society by merely deploring its evils — from the comfort of an arm-chair, or even from a pulpit. Someone once said, when comparing the great religions of the world 'Poor little Christianity — she talks too much'. A landmark in the Welsh border country is a copse of fir trees crowning a great hill. They were planted to commemorate one of Queen Victoria's jubilees; but someone has planted a further plot to commemorate the Silver Jubilee of Queen Elizabeth II. The action is worth a lot of talk about conservation.

The Christian cause needs more than passivity; the Kingdom of God is concerned with positive as well as negative virtues. For:

New occasions teach new duties,
Time makes ancient good uncouth,
They must upward still and onward
Who would keep abreast of truth.

CHARACTER IN CHANGING TIMES

2 Samuel

I wonder how many children's addresses you have heard on the call of Samuel? The story has long been a favourite for such occasions and so has its application — that you are never too young to hear the word of the Lord. And the message has sometimes been re-inforced by 'Hush'd was the evening hymn' set out to one of Sir Arthur Sullivan's soupier tunes!

But in fact the word 'child' has a wider reference in the Old Testament, and some scholars think that Samuel was a youth in late adolescence when he heard that call. Be that as it may; what the writer underlines is that Samuel stood close to God. And that ancient writer becomes our contemporary when he affirms the distinction between knowing about God and knowing God; he remains our contemporary when he implies that it is possible to be immersed in the things of God, and yet not to appreciate what those things are really about.

We looked last week at the changing times in which our three characters lived, and I suggested that you followed this course by reading the first ten chapters of I Samuel. I must say something about those chapters; for in them we have at least two traditions, two interpretations of events that have been woven together as a consecutive story. This is one reason for the inconsistencies of the narrative. We shall have to unravel this a bit more when we come to Saul. But it may have some effect on the varied way in which Samuel is presented.

He appears to have at least three quite distinctive roles. First, he is a priest and a judge — carrying on the work of Eli and his two sons, whose doom was revealed to him. Secondly, he is a statesman, responsible for establishing the kingdom of Israel, and for facilitating the choice of its first two kings. Thirdly, he is a prophet or seer, one who is to see into the will of God for his own generation and those which are to follow. The mind boggles if it tries to think of one person combining the offices of Prime Minister, Lord Chancellor, and Archbishop of Canterbury, but Chuch and State were one in Samuel's day and we have noted a possible reason for the different roles in which he appears. We will look now at each of them, and see how Samuel's exercise of each affected his attitude to change.

First, he was a judge. He represented the old order which was passing away, and was soon to be replaced. He didn't cling to that order, but at the same time, he didn't wash his hands of it and say 'Nothing can be done until the revolution comes.' Most of us work in conditions that are far from ideal. Most of us belong to churches that are far from ideal. Probably they always will be — though they might be a bit more ideal than they are! But all this must not prevent us from doing our best with what we have. Many people have done the finest work in cramping conditions. Let's not be sentimental about leaking school buildings or badly run businesses or dull churches. But let's be sure that even with bad tools, you can be a good workman. Many women in our Church feel justifiably bitter at being debarred from the priesthood; but that does not prevent them from exercising a valuable ministry. Samuel made the most of the past which he had inherited.

And he recognised the demands of the present. He accepted the idea of kingship with reluctance — for he saw the dangers and abuses to which it might lead. But he saw it as the answer for the times in which he lived. In the Church of England, we have some parallel in synodical government. Its disadvantages stand out a mile — the opportunities given to the bores, the proliferation of meetings, the sheer volume of words. Yet the time had come for our Church to be a more cohesive body. Sometimes we have to accept all the disadvantages of certain structures as the only way of getting things done in the present.

Here lies Samuel's most obvious contribution to Jewish history. He worked under the conditions of the old order. He brought into being a new order. But there is a third aspect of his work which is a bit more nebulous, yet in the end may be more significant than the other two. Under him, prophecy became part of the order of things. He became a national prophet, and he seems to have set up a school of prophets. In Israel's history, the prophet was to be a check on establishment. In all forms of society, we need that sort of check. We need to listen to those who criticise. Both in Church and State we have lived through times of rapid change, times of great upheaval. We often long for the business to stop. Perhaps we do need a period of stability. But, as Edmund Burke once wrote, 'A State without the means of some change is a state without the means of its conservation.'

What is true of the State is no less true of the Church. Samuel, who listened for the word of the Lord seems to have guessed this as he saw the need for the prophet. Prophets are necessary for our own age, as for any other; for they are the servants of the Holy Spirit whose very presence means continuous reformation.

CHARACTER IN CHANGING TIMES

3 Saul

Think of some of the dates in our history which seemed to usher in a time of promise. 1649 saw the execution of Charles I and it seemed to some a freedom from tyranny, so did 1660 when his son was restored. In our own century, 1918 and 1945 looked like the beginning of a new and better era. But always, in some way, hopes were to be disappointed. So it was with Israel's first King. Samuel took a flask of oil, and poured it over Saul's head and said,

'The Lord anoints you prince over his people Israel; you shall rule the people of the Lord and deliver them from the enemies round about them.' But the first book of Samuel ends with the death of the king after battle — a king already discredited, and a dynasty doomed.

We have thought of Eli who seemed to ignore the changes that were coming to his people, and of Samuel who was instrumental in bringing them to pass. Saul was the first to take advantage of them. But his character is very difficult to get at. For this, there are three reasons which we must now examine.

The first concerns the evidence. As we saw last week, there are at least two, possibly more, traditions, interpretations of the events that have been quite skilfully woven together in this book to make it read like a single narrative. But this accounts for its apparent inconsistencies. Take this matter of the choice of Saul. In chapter 10, Saul goes to see Samuel the prophet, and is chosen and anointed by him — in secret. Later in the same chapter, he is chosen by lot. Later still, he is chosen by popular acclaim. Again in the same book, the idea of kingship at one point seems at variance with the divine will, at another in accordance with it. This is the first reason why it is difficult to get at Saul.

The second concerns the religious taboos of the period. Here is one example. Saul was sent to destroy the Amalekites — utterly. But he spared Agag the king, and kept the best of the sheep and cattle. Our sympathies tend to be with Saul rather than with Samuel who had ordered this mass obliteration. And for this reason we may find it difficult to share the biblical estimate of Saul.

Thirdly, there is the matter of his illness. He was unbalanced. Great bursts of ecstasy were followed by great fits of melancholy. The writer speaks of an evil spirit coming upon Saul, and says that the Lord had forsaken him. We take a different view of mental illness. We are worried about how far Saul can be accounted responsible for some of his actions.

These then are three reasons why it is so difficult to get at Saul. Yet we have to take seriously the biblical account of him if we believe that the writers are trying to convey truth to us. And first we must notice the real assets and achievements of the man. He had tremendous physique — always a help to any leader. He got some way to establishing his kingdom; he extended his rule over Ephraim and Benjamin, and he gained some authority over Judah. Commentators vary in their estimate of how successful he was. His achievements were slight by comparison with those of David, but they were real achievements. And he remained immensely popular with his people right up to the time of his death and beyond it. Men risked their lives in order to give his body decent burial.

What went wrong? Prebenday Cleverley Ford in his study of Saul suggested that he seemed to lack the heart of religion — that he was careful about forms, strict about observances, but that the real thing was missing. For this view, which is surely the view that the writer of 1 Samuel wants us to take, he gives a number of examples. Let's just look at one — which I have already mentioned: the slaughter of the Amalekites. We saw how Saul kept the best of the sheep and cattle, which seems to us a wholly reasonable thing to do. He said it was for sacrifice; but could it have been also for gain? Was he an enlightened man, ahead of his age, disobeying taboos that were senseless, or was he seeing the whole business as one which could bring a profit?

History is full of illustrations of people who have used religion rather than followed it. Adolf Hitler was fond of claiming the protection of God, and tried to make the Lutheran Church a vehicle for his own propaganda. In my own lifetime, I have heard a revival of Christianity urged as a defence against Communism, or a remedy for crime. It could well be both. But you cannot so *use* the holy God whose love is around us and whose claims are upon us. God calls for our worship and service in his own right. He is not interested in a relationship with himself that is parallel to a marriage of convenience.

This is one lesson that we can learn from the biblical account of Saul. Another that we never dare forget is the substitution of forms and observances for the worship of the living God himself. The real test of our religion is whether it is more obedient to our Lord:

Oft did I with th' assembly join
And near thine altar drew,
A form of godliness was mine
The power I never knew.

So wrote Charles Wesley in a section of hymns significantly entitled 'Describing Formal Religion.'

I said that Eli spoke to the old in spirit. Samuel speaks to those at the height of their powers who can affect the society to which they belong. Saul speaks to younger people who see objectives and are tempted to manipulate people and principles in order to attain them.

There we could leave it — and him. But we won't. For Israel's kingship prepares us for the kingdom of Christ. Without Saul, there would be no David, and without David, no house to bear his name. The story of Israel's kings is like the story of heroes in every age. We see great men, gifted men, but always men with some flaw in them. We see that there is One and One only to whom we may give our allegiance. And it is the Lord of mercy who is the Lord of judgement. So Browning looks forward:

O Saul, it shall be
A face like my face that receives thee: a man like to me,
Thou shalt love and be loved by, for ever: a Hand like this Hand
Shall throw open the gates of new life to thee!
See the Christ stand!

INDIVDUAL SERMONS

1 The Second Chance

Luke 13. 6–9

Towards the end of the last century, a farmer made a packet of money, and decided that he would go on his travels. When he got to Rome, he was shown some chickens, and told that they were descendants of the cock that had crowed on the night of Peter's betrayal. He was unmoved by this piece of information, and merely enquired 'Be they good layers?'

This is the point of the little parable of the barren fig tree. It tells us at least three things about God's dealings with us: that he is a God of purpose, that he is a God of judgement, and that he is a God of forbearance.

He is a God of purpose. His purpose for the fig tree was that it should bear figs. His purpose for us, and for the society to which we belong is that we should be fruitful. I wonder whether we have really taken this in. We are apt to think that provided we refrain from the more glaring sins, provided we try to exercise a few virtues, we can get through life in a way that ought to be acceptable to God. The parable tells us that this is not so. In the first chapters of the Bible, we are told that when God created the world in six days, he rested on the seventh. We are not told that he has been resting ever since. Indeed, we see him now as an endless source of creativity, and creation as a process that is still going on. A great cathedral still needs an architect, for there is always some part of it in need of renewal. God has a purpose for his whole creation that has yet to be fulfilled; and his purpose is that each part of it should attain that perfection which is his design for it.

So he must be a God of judgement. The fig tree didn't bear fruit. That was one reason why the owner wanted it cut down. But there was another. It cumbered the ground. It took up soil that might have been used more profitably. Maybe it did harm to the ground by sucking in goodness to no avail. Natural history is full of instances of forms of life that have died out. Human history tells of empires that have decayed and disappeared. Church history records forms of religion or expressions of Christianity that have become moribund. Now often the reasons for all this change and decay are complicated. But the point of the parable stands: that uselessness brings its own judgement. The parable was addressed to a society in which church and state were one; Israel made the persistent mistake of supposing that she enjoyed the divine protection — whatever she did. So sometimes does the Church of today. One of the our present dangers is that we become little in-groups; but unless we are ministering the love of God to those outside our number, we are like the barren fig tree bearing no fruit.

This judgement we must understand. But this has been called the parable of the second chance. Our God is a God of for-bearance. And of all three things that the story tells us about God, this is the most important. He longs that we shall turn to him; he longs that we shall turn out to the world in mission and service. He uses every opportunity to bring this love home to us. He gives us every chance to change our outlook. The digging and dunging of the parable can be paralleled by what we sometimes call 'the means of grace' — worship and sacrament, prayer and the study of the scriptures. All these are meant to equip and strengthen us for what we ought to be doing. For God loves us as he loves his ancient people. He wants for us to be what he knows we can be.

I'd like to remind you of an ancient prayer that was for some years used on the Sunday that this parable was read in church. Many people have lived and been nourished by the collects of the Prayer Book. But this one was heard only in the years when Easter was late-ish. The collect of the fourth Sunday after Epiphany ran:

> O god, who knowest us to be set in the midst of so many and great dangers that by reason of the frailty of our nature, we cannot always stand upright; Grant to us such strength and protection as may support us in all dangers and carry us through all temptations; through Jesus Christ our Lord.

The address has a sense of the divine understanding that you don't always find in the reformers of the sixteenth century. Much earlier than that, Brother Lawrence used to say when he failed — 'I shall never do otherwise if I am left to myself.' God knows that we fail, but He is always there to help us stand up again. So the collect goes on to ask for help in dangers and temptations — not just those which are obvious, but the temptations of sloth, of cynicism, of despair or of that judgement upon other people which forgets that we also are under judgement.

Let that prayer enable us to make the most of the second chance

— to take it, to rejoice in it, to use it. For if the story of the world around us is enough to cast us down, the story of our faith is enough to raise us up. For through it we know that what is evil can be redeemed, what seems to be in decay can be renewed, what looks dead can be brought to resurrection.

INDIVIDUAL SERMONS

2 Advice

1 Kings 12. 1–20

The trouble about asking advice is that it's often very difficult not to take it. Well might the writer of the book that we call Ecclesiasticus say:

'Accept a greeting from everyone, but advice from
only one in a thousand.'

But if you disobey that recommendation, and take it from two in a thousand and the two pieces of advice are contradictory, then you're really in trouble because you're bound to offend someone.

That is what happened to Rehoboam, king of Israel. He turned first to the venerable counsellors of his father's reign, and then to the people who belonged to his own age group. As we read in the story, he rejected the advice of the first and accepted that of the second.

And he was wrong. There is no doubt where the sympathies of the writer of 1 Kings lay; but then he had to explain why it was that the great kingdom of David and Solomon so soon fell apart. He had to show why Rehoboam could not hold it together. He paints a pretty unattractive picture of the new king and his circle — they look a hard-faced lot, a Fascist lot. On the evidence of the story not many right-minded people would have much sympathy for Rehoboam and his arrogant young friends. There is no doubt that the advice of the old men was both more humane and more sane. They told him to win his subjects. He chose to force them.

99

It's a story of youth and age. It doesn't mean that the old are always right and the young always wrong — a few pages back in the Bible, you find that the young man David is the hero of the story. But since the writer lays stress on the age of those who gave advice, let's look at what it is that age and youth have to offer when it comes to decision-making. But first let's be sure that this is a bit relative, this matter of youth and age. There are sage young people and immature old people. There was once a youth leader who used to talk about the 'old women of both sexes'. He might have added 'and of all ages'.

But in general, youth has the advantage of identifying issues, seeing objectives. It can also be impatient of compromise and ignorant of obstacles. Often it sees more clearly what should be done than how to do it. Age has often learned to settle for much less than it would have originally chosen. It has become more adroit at handling situations and understanding people. But means have sometimes become more important than ends, and aims get a bit clouded in the process.

When it comes to the matter of decisions, somehow we need the advice of both. We need those who see what ought to be done, and see through the lethargy and hypocrisy that often cause them not to be done. Robert Louis Stevenson once wrote, 'For God's sake give me the young man who has brains enough to make a fool of himself.'

A group of young clergy was recently discussing whether the leaders of the Church ought to make a pronouncement on a certain social issue. One said 'We might be misunderstood' and another replied 'There are always good reasons for keeping quiet when something ought to be said.'

We need the vision of youth. Yet it can get distorted — as with Rohoboam and his friends, as with the Hitler Youth Movement in the nineteen-thirties, as with gangs who roam our streets today. So we need also the politics of age — of people who can tell us how to live to fight another day, how to treat people in order to gain the objectives that have been perceived.

Maybe someone is getting impatient with this talk of the contributions of youth and age, and of the wordly wisdom that may seem to lie behind it. Surely it's not the vision of the young or the wisdom of the aged that we should be seeking in our decisions, but the will of God? Isn't that where the Church should be looking? And isn't that what we should be praying for when we think of any who have great decisions to make?

Most assuredly, yes. But God has caused us to live in families, in societies in this world, and we are meant to learn of him by learning from our fellows. Of course we must pray for guidance, and try to listen for the living word of God, but never suppose that we then have a monopoly of divine wisdom.

There are Christians who have thought that they had. Abraham Lincoln said, 'I am approached with the most opposite opinions and advice, and that by religious men, who are equally certain that they represent the divine will.'

He went on to say that he did not always receive direct revelation, and therefore, 'I must study the plain physical facts of the case, ascertain what is possible, and learn what appears to be wise and right.'

So what about those decisions that we have to make? We must ask for guidance — aware that our powers of self-deception are considerable. We must ask to be as free as possible from those prejudices which may close our mind to any but one course of action. We may seek advice of those through whom God can help us — asking not 'What should I do?' but 'What would You do', and then choose the course of action that seems to us nearest to the way of Christ. The decision must be ours, for God wills it to be so. When you counsel other people, it is not to tell them what to do, but to help them to make up their own minds. 'I have not called you servants but friends' we read in St John's Gospel, and this is the clue to that status which has been conferred upon us. With all that we can make our decisions — modestly, yet with confidence.

INDIVIDUAL SERMONS

3 Old and New

St Matthew 13. 52 When therefore a teacher of the law has become a learner in the Kingdom of God, he is like a householder who can produce from his store both the new and the old.

In November 1979 the General Synod of the Church of England received a petition with six hundred signatories; broadly speaking, it asked for continued use of the Book of Common Prayer and the Authorised Version of the Bible. There were some bitter words about the new services; and there were laudations of the old ones by people who never attended them. But there were some who recognised the need for changes, for experiments, for alternatives, and asked for no more than the retention of the old alongside the new. This was the Synod which arranged the final details of the Alternative Service Book.

Jesus told a tiny parable of a householder who could indeed bring forth out of his store both the new and the old. We can picture such a man today. He is one who loves old silver yet sees the value of modern stainless steel. Perhaps he uses old country remedies, but appreciates all that medicine has discovered about anaesthetics. He knows the beauty of old English oak, yet can find a place for modern designs in teak. There are many such people. You can find antique shops in unlikely industrial villages; but those who buy from them usually like to have up-to-date fittings in their kitchen or bathroom.

Of course the parable has a context. There was some tension in the early Church between the new Gospel and the old Law. Circumcision became an issue for this reason. And of all the evangelists, Matthew seems most concerned to show that Jesus' life, death and resurrection were in accordance with the message of the ancient scriptures, that he had come not to destroy the Law, but to fulfil it.

Those controversies are now long passed, but the parable still has something to say about the policy of the Church and the attitudes of its members. The 'old' which we now have consists not only of our Jewish inheritance in the Old Testament, but of our Christian inheritance of the last two thousand years. We have the work of people who wrestled to understand and express the Faith; of the spiritual writers who explored how men and women could live as God's children; of those who sought to expound the things of God in art and words and music. The 'new' with which we are now concerned is the work of all those who continue to do these things — to search for the contemporary meaning of doctrine, to look for the will and purpose of God in situations very different from those in which the New Testament was set, to find prayers and praise appropriate to people who are alive now, to offer their own artistic skills in the service of God. Undergirding all this is the belief that the God who led his people in past centuries is the One who is leading them now; that the Holy Spirit who spoke through men and women of old is the Holy Spirit who is still revealing the truth of God and guiding us to understand it.

We began with the petition presented to the General Synod, so let us try to understand what all this might mean in the sensitive area of worship. It means, in the first place, that we shall value the heritage of the past. We shall not dismiss those ancient and basic symbols which spoke to our forefathers — symbols of water, or oil or light, movements of the body expressive of certain features of worship, or the tradition that all its senses must be involved. We shall see, too, the beauty of language and design. And whilst we remember the linguistic glories of the Authorised Version and the Prayer Book, we shall not forget those of other centuries — like the hymns of Wesley and Watts and some of their contemporaries, which made the eighteenth century one of the greatest in the history of congregational praise.

But secondly, we shall see with Benjamin Jowett, that 'We can never have the faith of our fathers because the light will always be breaking in upon us.' We shall rejoice that scholarship has illuminated our understanding of the scriptures, that scientific study has changed our view of the world, that psychological study has affected our understanding of human nature. All these things we shall want to reflect in our worship — which must be related to

103

our understanding of God's continual revelation of himself. Some things that we want to say have already been well said for us; some things we want to say in the words of our time. So alongside the classic prayers and praises of Christendom will be the new prayers and new hymns which have made the last twenty years so creative a period in the history of Christian worship.

There is no reason why the two should not exist side by side, and why we should not use them like that wise householder who could produce from his treasure both the new and the old. For we do need both; I imagine that not even the most devoted admirer of the Prayer Book would want to be confined to the forms provided for the Visitation of the Sick within its covers; and I cannot believe that the most enthusiastic supporter of modern liturgy would want to banish for ever the General Thanksgiving or Wesley's 'Love divine'. In a pamphlet on the language of Series III, David Frost pointed out that we do not find it incongruous to walk along a street in which Tudor, Georgian and Victorian houses are mingled; and it is the same with liturgy. There is no need for a 'pistols at dawn' attitude over the language of worship.

For what a storehouse we have! Let us revel in the things that are there, and in the things that are still being brought in. Let us be discriminating about what we use now, and wise enough to leave some things there for another day. This is the way for us who remain learners in the Kingdom of God.

INDIVIDUAL SERMONS

4 Prejudice

St Luke 10. 33 But a Samaritan who was making the journey came upon him, and when he saw him, was moved to pity.

If you go on an organised tour to Israel, you will probably spend part of your time in Galilee, and part in Jerusalem. A route between the two leads through Nablus, and you will be shown on the outskirts, Jacob's Well, where Jesus once talked with a Samaritan woman. But it is not always possible to go this way, for Nablus has long been a centre of unrest. There, in some strange way, history is repeating itself; for this is ancient Samaria.

We have read the parable of the Good Samaritan. It was recorded by a Jew, and written down for Jews; and these facts are remarkable when you remember that Jews and Samaritans hated each other. Why they did so is a complicated story. Doubtless political and economic reasons divided them. But by the time of Jesus, they believed different things about God. True, both accepted the first five books of the Bible, and both accepted Moses, the servant of the Lord. But after this, they differed. The Samaritans had no other Scriptures; the Jews had the prophets and the other writings. The Samaritans had a more static view of God; he had once revealed himself, but now was absent. The Jews had a more dynamic view of God; he was constantly intervening in human history. Try to think of a Christianity that not only neglects the Holy Spirit, but actually disbelieves in him — and you have a rough idea of Samaritan religion. Maybe it's not so strange as it sounds. One of the contributors to *The Myth of God Incarnete* suggested that orthodox formulations of the doctrine of the Incarnation bear traces of Samaritan influence.

No doubt the feud between Jews and Samaritans was kept alive by people who had no idea of its origins. Divisions always thrive on ignorance. Divisions between people who have much in common can be very bitter — and to this, the story of Christian disunity bears tragic testimony. In Jesus' time, the very word 'Samaritan' was banned wherever possible; you notice that at the end of the story, the lawyer carefully refrains from using it. The evidence of Samaritans was inadmissable in Jewish courts; in the synagogues, they were publicly cursed. Probably no greater insult was offered to Jesus than the one recorded in St John's Gospel — 'Say we not well that thou are a Samaritan and hast a devil?'

Here in St Luke's Gospel, there are three references to Samaritans — which might be expected of a writer who had great interest in non-Jewish peoples. The first is conventional enough.

Jesus passes through their territory, but is not received — because he is on his way to Jerusalem. Luke has no illusions. But the other two references make the Samaritan hero of the story. There is the parable of the Good Samaritan; there is the story of how ten men were cured of leprosy, but only one showed real gratitude. That one was a Samaritan.

Before we go on to ask what Luke is saying to us, we must be clear about what he is *not* saying. He is *not* saying that it doesn't matter what you believe, so long as you do good. He is a Jew, and he does find Samaritan religion defective. He is *not* saying that actions are all that matters; directly after the story of the Good Samaritan comes that of Martha and Mary, where willingness to listen is rated as equal to practical service.

But he is telling us to recognise good in people who differ from us. We never want to. We tend to rejoice when moral weakness is found in those whose convictions are opposed to our own. We are seldom able to recognise good in our opponents. We put labels on people. Doubtless there is more than meets the eye in Housman's poem, but it is not untypical of human attitudes:

> Oh, who is that young sinner with the handcuffs on his wrists?
> And what has he been after that they groan and shake their fists?
> And wherefore is he wearing such a conscience-stricken air?
> Oh, they're taking him to prison for the colour of his hair.
>
> 'Tis a shame to human nature, such a head of hair as his;
> In the good old time 'twas hanging for the colour that it is;
> Though hanging isn't bad enough and flaying would be fair
> For the nameless and abominable colour of his hair.

In his autobiography *Crowded Canvas*, Max Warren, for so many years the revered General Secretary of the Church Missionary Society, recalled that when he went up to Cambridge, he came under the influence of the Franciscans, and as a raw Evangelical came to see that Christ could be found even in an Anglo-Catholic! Luke invites us to see good in those from whom we differ on quite radical points.

He wants us to do more. Not only are we to see the good that is in our opponents, but we are to imitate it. The Samaritan may have got only half the truth about God's revelation, but at least he practised the good that he knew. What he did on that desolate road that leads from Jerusalem to Jericho is what any Jew ought to have done. Time and again members of the Christian Church are put to shame by those who do not share their convictions, or enjoy their privileges. We began by referring to organised tours of Israel. Those arranged by Inter-Church Travel usually have a large proportion of practising Christians. On one such, one man was an avowed atheist. He never attended the prayers held each evening. But it was he who thought of buying a thank-you card for the leader, and collecting signatures.

It was like the story of the ten lepers. But in *this* story when the lawyer gave the only possible answer to Jesus' question, he was told 'Go, and do as he did.'

APPENDIX I

Abbreviations: AMR   Hymns Ancient and Modern Revised
                 EH   English Hymnal
                 HFT   One Hundred Hymns for Today
                 WOV   With One Voice

SUGGESTIONS FOR RELATING THESE SERMONS TO THEIR CONTEXT IN WORSHIP

The Introduction has emphasised that the sermon should be related to the other variable parts of worship. In normal practice, this means the lectionary, the hymns and the prayers. The lectionary will usually determine the theme of the sermon. The more flexible forms of intercession provided by the modern orders of the Eucharist are encouraging a reflection of themes from the sermon in the prayers. But the hymns are often only vaguely related to it. Where a hymn directly follows the sermon, it should be a response of the congregation to the Word that has been preached; and even at the Eucharist, where much happens between sermon and hymn, its themes can be taken up in those sung at the Offertory or after Communion.

I make no attempt (except in one illustration) to draw up complete lists of hymns in connection with these sermons, since they were intended for a variety of occasions, and with different lectionaries in use. This appendix merely suggests hymns that arise from the sermon, and (in one case) some points of prayer that could help in the planning of services.

If the Advent course were used at the Eucharist, the hymns for the first Sunday would be the most general on the coming of Christ — *O come, O come Emmanuel* (AMR 49), *The Advent of our God* (EH 11), *Hark, a thrilling voice is sounding* (AMR 47). The second Sunday would have hymns on the Bible, but could include one on the earthly life of Jesus like *Son of the Lord most high* (HFT 87). Both the Book of Common Prayer and the New Lectionary emphasise the role of John the Baptist on the third Sunday; but in addition to *On Jordan's Bank* (AMR 50), *Hark! the glad sound* (AMR 53) would fit our theme; so would *We find thee Lord in others need* (HFT 97), and at the Offertory *Lord enthroned in heavenly splendour* (AMR 400) because of the third verse. *The Lord will come and not be slow* (AMR 52) and *Lo! He come with clouds descending* (AMR 51) would be appropriate to the sermon called 'The Christ who will come.' This is a season when forward-planning of the hymns is helpful — since it is possible to sing all the best on the first Sunday, and to have a second-rate remainder for the next three!

Christmas hymns tend to choose themselves, but even here there is room for variety in the selection and order. Nothing precisely takes up the interpretation of the role of the shepherds offered here — *While shepherds watched* (AMR 62) simply retells Luke 2 without comment. Some verses of *Christians awake!* (AMR 61) would be appropriate; and if the sermon is preached at the Midnight Eucharist, and the Offertory comes after midnight, there is no reason why the whole of that superb hymn should not then be sung. The last two verses, as printed in Hymns Ancient and Modern Revised make an excellent close to a Christmas service.

There is a dearth of good modern hymns for Lent, and those which deal with fasting often sound unreal or exaggerated. The sermon for Ash Wednesday would need those which speak positively of discipline. As to the course offered Psalm 90 obviously suggests Watts' famous paraphrase — even better if it is sung with the original pronoun *Our God our help in ages past* (AMR 165); *How shall I sing that majesty* (EH 404) would be good at the beginning of the service and *Now is eternal life* (HFT 69) at the close. The exposition of Psalm 49 is reflected in *Son of God, Eternal Saviour* (AMR 207), and in *God of Grace and God of Glory* (HFT 34). Psalm 51 has a metrical version in many hymn books, and *Jesu Lover of my Soul* (especially with the great third verse printed in EH 414) can be sung alongside it. *All my hope* (HFT 3) could accompany Psalm 121, and so could *Sing praise to God* (AMR 366). Psalm 148 suggests hymns of praise — like *Let all the world* (AMR 375).

The original setting of the Passiontide sermons was mentioned in the Introduction. The order of each half-hour was: Readings, address, silence, hymn, prayers, organ music — and such comings and goings as there were took place at the end of the appropriate voluntary in each section. The hymns for each address were *God is love* (HFT 32), *O Sacred Head* (EH 102), *When I survey* (EH 107) and *Lift up your heads, ye gates of brass* (EH 549).

An Easter service would obviously include the two hymns quoted in the sermon itself. Among the Ascension-tide hymns would be *Alleluia sing to Jesus* (AMR 399) which is much over-worked but particularly suitable to this theme. Pentecost would include hymns which describe the manifold activity of the Spirit as well as those which invoke him; deserving to be much better known is *Our Lord, his Passion ended* (AMR 155), but useful also is *O Holy Ghost, thy people bless* (AMR 234).

I suggest one hymn for the sermons for special groups, as much of the material in such services is likely to be predetermined: *Lord of all power* (HFT 62) for teachers, *The Head that once was crowned with thorns* (AMR 218) for nurses, *Lord Christ, who on thy heart* (HFT 55) for mothers, and *Eternal ruler* (HFT 20) for minorities. Nineteenth century missionary hymns are not now likely to be chosen for a missionary festival, and will probably be replaced by more timeless material like *Jesus shall reign* (AMR 220). Harvest Thanksgiving obviously demands some of the 'old favourites', but it is sad if this occasion annually leaves people exactly where they were before; some note of dedication as well as thanksgiving is required here; *Praise and thanksgiving* (HFT 82) helps to supply it, and so does material from other supplements. The same con-siderations apply to Remembrance Sunday which surely calls for hymns on World Peace (see the section in HFT) rather than the jingoistic offerings of a generation ago or the much too general material suggested by the present official forms of service. The sermon for an Arts Festival suggests *God moves in a mysterious way*

(EH 394) and *God is a name my soul adores* (WOV 31) which is at last beginning to be found in some books used by Anglicans.

The sermon on Eli could be followed by *Once to every man and nation* (EH 563) if available, or *Father hear the prayer we offer* (AMR 182). *Hush'd was the evening hymn* has gone into limbo as far as most congregations are concerned and, in any case, the treatment of Samuel offered here would be better served by *O day of God, draw nigh* (HFT 72) or, *Ye servants of the Lord* (EH 518). With a word of explanation *Hail to the Lord's Anointed* (AMR 219) could well be associated with the sermon on Saul — as could *Lift up your hearts* (AMR 341) or, *Be thou my vision* (HFT 10). The last two could be used with the sermon called 'The Second Chance', as could *O breath of life, come sweeping through us* (WOV 322). For 'Old and New' it would be worth duplicating Erik Routley's fine paraphrase of Psalm 98 — *New songs of celebration render* (New Church Praise 66), or even, as an object lesson, reviving the first hymn Isaac Watts is said to have written:

> Behold the glories of the Lamb
> Amidst his Father's throne:
> Prepare new honours for his Name,
> And songs before unknown.

I mentioned in the Introduction that the sermon on Prejudice was appropriate to Pentecost 16 (New Lectionary — Year I). By way of further illustration, I therefore suggest hymns for that Sunday, and material for the five sections of the intercession:

> Introit: *God of mercy, God of grace* (AMR 264)
> Gradual: *Jesus, Lord, we look to Thee* (HFT 47)
> Offertory: *For the healing of the nations* (HFT 28)
> Postcommunion: *Jesus shall reign* (AMR 220)

'Guide your Church in its relations with people of different faiths. We remember with sorrow Christian persecution of others, and we pray for your ancient people. . .

Hear us as remember our own multi-racial society, as we think of opposing political parties, of management and workers. . .

Help us to recognise good in those with whom we find it hard to live, whether at home or at work. . .

Bless all who minister to every kind of human need; the work of the Samaritans, of voluntary as well as state services. Sharpen our own insight and sensitivity. . .

To you who alone are Judge, we commit the souls of the those who have died; and we thank you for men and women of every creed who have reflected your light and love. . .'

But if on the same Sunday and with the same readings, the sermon were more directly related to the Epistle, and its theme 'Sympathy' the same hymns and prayers might 'do', but others would be better:

> Introit: *Where high the heavenly temple stands* (AMR 204)
> Gradual: *We find thee, Lord, in others need* (HFT 97)
> Offertory: *Son of God, eternal Saviour* (AMR 207)
> Post-communion: *Praise the Lord, raise up rejoicing* (HFT 83)

'Give us the grace of sympathy as we think of our fellow Christians, of those whose traditions and circumstances are so different from our own. . .

As we pray for our leaders in nation, in industry or the social service. . .

As we pray for those whom we meet every day at work or at home, those who live around us, those who belong to this church. . .

As we remember every form of human need; the lonely and the bereaved; those whom we find it hard to approach; those who themselves find it hard to communicate with us. . .

To your searching compassion we commit the souls of those who have died, those who now face death. . . '

APPENDIX II

A SHORT BIBLIOGRAPHY

Of the recent major books on preaching I select three. In *The Ministry of the Word* by D. W. Cleverley Ford (Hodder and Stoughton 1979) we have an expansion of those writings which have helped so many preachers during the last twenty years — including those who attended the courses of the College of Preachers — of which the author was so long the distinguished Director. Colin Morris' *The Word and the Words* (Epworth 1975) is a penetrating analysis of the place of preaching, and will appeal to those who are sceptical as well as to those who are convinced of its value. *A Guide to Preaching* by R. E. O. White (Pickering and Inglis 1973), is an intensely practical book, necessary not only for those who are beginning to preach, but for whose who think they know how to do so.

The choice of books of sermons is essentially personal, and I have been helped by many that are not listed here. In secondhand bookshops, the various volumes of F. W. Robertson are worth picking up. So are *A Great View* by Eric Loveday (Skeffington & Son 1952) and the two volumes by Bernard Manning — *A Layman in the Ministry* and *More Sermons of a Layman* (both Independant Press 1952). In more recent times there is *Windsor Sermons* by Alec Vidler (SCM 1963). Most preachers of my generation will have *The True Wilderness* by H. A. Williams (Constable 1965) and *The Shaking of the Foundations* by Paul Tillich (Pelican 1963); To these could be added *Strength to Love* by Martin Luther King (Fontana 1969). Karl Barth is well represented by *Call for God* (SCM 1967). From Epworth Press I have particularly valued *Aflame with Faith* by Donald Soper (1963), *Saul among the Prophets* by Erik Routley (1971) and *The Sixty Plus and Other Sermons* by Gordon Rupp (1978). Too numerous to list are the many collections of D. W. Cleverley Ford — both those in this series and those of earlier years.

Besides indispensable theological material, books of reference of many kinds, including dictionaries of quotations, are of constant value to the preacher. Of outstanding use to me is *A Treasury of Quotations on Christian Themes* by Carroll E. Simcox (SPCK 1976) and to a lesser extent William Neil's *Concise Dictionary of Religious Quotations* (Mowbrays 1975). And I envy the discipline of some of my friends who have commonplace books, and keep them up to date.